# So *you* Want to *follow* Jesus?

## 15 QUESTIONS FOR WOULD-BE DISCIPLES

## STAN MEEK

Packaged by WinePress Publishing, PO Box 428, Enumclaw, WA 98022. The views expressed or implied in this work do not necessarily reflect those of WinePress Publishing. The author is ultimately responsible for the design, content and editorial accuracy of this work.



Unless otherwise noted, all Scriptures are taken from the Holy Bible, *New International Version*, Copyright © 1973, 1978, 1984 by the International Bible Society. Used by permission of Zondervan Publishing House. The "NIV" and "New International Version" trademarks are registered in the United States Patent and Trademark Office by International Bible Society.

Scripture references marked KJV are taken from the *King James Version* of the Bible.

Scripture references marked TLB are taken from *The Living Bible*, © 1971 owned by assignment by Illinois Regional Bank N.A. (as trustee). Used by permission of Tyndale House Publishers, Inc., Wheaton, Illinois 60189. All rights reserved.

Scripture references marked THE MESSAGE are taken from *The Message Bible* © 1993 by Eugene N. Peterson, NavPress, POB 35001, Colorado Springs, CO 80935, 4th printing in USA 1994. Published in association with the literary agency—Aline Comm. POB 49068, Colorado Springs, CO 80949. Used by permission.

Scripture references marked CEV are taken from *The Contemporary English Version*: Thomas Nelson, 1997, c1995 by the American Bible Society. Used by permission. All rights reserved.

ISBN 1-57921-731-1
Library of Congress Catalog Card Number: 2003115746

"Stan Meek captured the questions and concerns of new believers. In responding to their questions he taps the rich resources of the Bible and capable Christian writers."

—Lyle B. Pointer
Professor of Evangelism
Nazarene Theological Seminary

"Stan Meek's book, *So You Want to Follow Jesus?* is an answer to a pastor's prayers. It will help those who are 'born in the Lord,' to 'mature in the Lord.' This is a great tool for those who want to experience God's best in their lives."

—Gene & Joyce Williams
Authors & Directors of
Shepherd's Fold Ministries
Wichita, Kansas

"What a wonderful resource to reach an unchurched culture. With 7 out of 10 people in America not going to church anywhere, this timely book will be a handy incentive to encourage church attenders to evangelize."

—Stan Toler
Author & Pastor
Oklahoma City, Oklahoma

"Once again Stan Meek has found a way to address an issue that we've all considered but done nothing about. His style is so 'readable' that it makes tough questions easy to digest, yet challenges the reader to be a true disciple of Jesus Christ."

—Tim Stearman, Pastor
First Church of the Nazarene
Denver, Colorado

"The richness of *So You Want to Follow Jesus?* makes it a tremendously valuable resource for the believer who takes the Master's call to discipleship seriously. It is Scripturally sound, intensely practical, and warm in tone, which makes for easy reading. Rev. Meek has a rare gift for providing clear usable steps for being a true disciple."

—Russell Human
District Superintendent Emeritus
Church of the Nazarene

"I have looked for a book like this for a long time. I can foresee that *So You Want to Follow Jesus?* is going to be a useful and popular book for both Christians and inquirers. The 15 topics are so essential."

—Amy Lin
Education Pastor
Evangelical Formosan Church
Irvine, California

"Stan Meek has forged a well-documented primer for believers that will be of great value to any serious new follower of Christ. The use of fresh metaphors skillfully mixed with quotations from Christian thinkers along with a pastor's experience and insight fashion a vital bridge to enable believers to become disciples in contemporary culture. All this in easy to understand language."

—Max Jetton
Pastor
Yorba Linda, California

"At a time when Christian growth and discipleship need to be emphasized, *So You Want to Follow Jesus?* will be an invaluable resource. The insightful study and accompanying questions will challenge believers to apply themselves toward both *being* and *making* disciples."

—-Mark Tincher, Senior Pastor
First Church of God
Pryor Creek, Oklahoma

"The cost of discipleship is high, and the journey is difficult. For new Christians, it can seem overwhelming. *So You Want to Follow Jesus?* is a wonderful resource for helping new believers take their first steps. Without compromise, it breaks discipleship down into manageable components. I can envision this book as an effective tool here in Italy to help first-time believers discover a truly Christ-centered lifestyle of discipleship."

—Joel Mullen
Missionary
Palermo, Italy

To our children, grandchildren, and great-grandchildren, with
prayers that each of them will discover the joy of becoming
true disciples of our Lord Jesus Christ.

# CONTENTS

# Appendix

# ACKNOWLEDGMENTS

My heartfelt appreciation to my wife, Patricia Elizabeth, whose faith in God and in me has been a constant strength and encouragement. Her love, patience, and wisdom have made me a better disciple and a better writer.

Special thanks to Dr. Lyle Pointer, whose encouragement and personal interest in my writing have kept me on the stretch to reach my goals. I am also grateful to Mark Gilroy for his wise counsel in regard to the publishing and marketing of books.

I am especially grateful to Athena Dean and Janice Robeson at WinePress Publishers for their kind, patient, and expert guidance in regard to the publishing of this book. I salute the entire WinePress family. We are honored to partner with you for the glory of God.

Recognition is also given to *Herald of Holiness*, *Holiness Today*, and to Beacon Hill Press for use of some material previously published in these journals, and in the dialog study book, *How To Improve Your Prayer Life.*

The reader will find that the text of *So You Want to Follow Jesus?* is heavily laced with gems of wisdom from great Christian minds of today and from the past. I have chosen to liberally "showcase" these diamonds and rubies of truth regarding the journey of discipleship. Their impact upon my life has been substantial.

I have attempted to work very carefully regarding documentation of materials quoted. If I have failed to give proper credit to any source, it would definitely be only an oversight.

# INTRODUCTION

In September of the last year of the second millennium (1999), a historic meeting took place in the South of England—The First International Consultation on Discipleship.

That gathering of some 450 Christian leaders, representing 70 organizations from 50 countries focused on a growing concern: Although the church is registering many converts, the making of disciples lags far behind.

*So You Want to Follow Jesus?* is one effort to address this problem, with the goal of turning believers into disciples. Often we assume that people are aware of the cost and the basics of discipleship, but they are not. They need simple instruction and guidance in everyday language regarding many things that Christians and "churched" persons in previous generations understood more readily.

And discipleship is difficult. Oswald Chambers says, "following in the steps of Jesus in discipleship is so great a mystery that few enter into it."[1] But like all of the "hard sayings" of Jesus, the truth remains a mystery only to those who refuse to obey and choose to remain blind.

Jesus called persons to know Him and to follow Him, but He never made following Him easy. And honest seekers and serious followers, today and in the past, have always asked questions like: "What will following Jesus mean?" "What determines the kind of follower I will be?" "Will I have the power that I need to follow Jesus?" "Is there a secret to persevering in the faith?" "What shall I do when I've failed God?" "What about the church?" "Can I find that perfect church?" "When is discipleship successful?" "Will God's grace be good enough?" Thought-provoking answers to such questions comprise the stuff of this book.

Following Jesus is *discipleship*, and discipleship is difficult, not because it is not understood, but because it is *costly*, and few are willing to pay the price. In the new millennium, will following Jesus really change that much, or is discipleship *discipleship*, whether it is Peter and John following Jesus in the First Century or Roy and Ron following Jesus in the Twenty-First Century?

Dallas Willard says "When Jesus walked among humankind there was a certain simplicity to being his disciple. Primarily it meant to go with him, in an attitude of study, obedience, and imitation. There were no correspondence courses. One knew what to do and what it would cost . . . disciples had to be with him to learn how to do what he did . . . the mechanics are not the same today," says Willard, "we cannot literally be with him in the same way as his first disciples could. But the priorities and intentions—the heart or inner attitudes of disciples are forever the same."[2] The core of discipleship, the author believes, will remain the same. To be quite sure, the culture has changed radically, and will continue to change. Most likely the rate and nature of change in the new millennium will be dizzying and astounding beyond our imagination.

These changes will undoubtedly affect the way we give expression to our basic personal faith, and call forth from third-millennium Christians adjustments and applications of that faith that are yet unseen. Still, the core issues of following Jesus remain. If one masters these essentials, he or she can not only survive, but thrive spiritually regardless of the changes in the culture.

This book will not attempt to examine in any depth the nature of changes the new millennium may bring, but will examine rather the fundamentals of following Jesus, requisite for any age—what might be called *mere discipleship*.

William Dembski, editor of *Mere Creation: Science, Faith, and Intelligent Design*, engaged my mind. He wrote: "Sticking *mere* in front of a concept can be a way of trivializing it . . . sticking 'mere' in front of a concept can, however, also be a way of getting at its essentials. Thus for C. S. Lewis, 'mere Christianity' signified the essentials of Christianity, what minimally one must hold to be a Christian."[3]

It was in the second sense that Dembski and his scholarly authors advanced the theory of "intelligent design" regarding the origins of our world. It is in this second sense also that this author advances the concept of following Jesus as *mere* discipleship, or a *default* discipleship as perhaps this "computer generation" would prefer to think of it.

Willard reminds us, "the disciple of Jesus is not the deluxe or heavy-duty model of the Christian—especially padded, textured, streamlined, and empowered for the fast lane on the straight and narrow way. He stands on the pages of the New Testament as the first level of basic transportation in the Kingdom of God."[4] God wants *every* Christian believer to be a real disciple.

We once had installed a waterline on our property that required digging a ditch and then refilling it. Since we have rocky northeast Oklahoma soil, our grandson was helping us to pick up little rocks and place them in a pile. His grandmother had showed him that not everything that looks like a rock is in fact a real rock. She explained that some were only clods that looked like rock until you banged them against something hard, like another rock.

Occasionally the grandson would call out, "Grandmother, is this a *real* rock? And he would pound away. Many forces, and some unidentified stresses in the new millennium, will be pounding away on our Christian faith trying to discover whether or not we are *real* Christians. *So You Want to Follow Jesus?* gets to the heart of what it means to truly follow Jesus in any time frame.

Our ideas regarding discipleship must, of course, be Biblically and theologically sound. One cannot afford to be wrong about something that demands "my life, my love, my all." The author believes, however, that the ordinary Christian does not want this information to come to him or her in heavy theological garb, but in simple, easy to understand, everyday language.

Today's Christians want someone who's "been there and done that" to tell them how to get to the heart of discipleship—how to live the Christian life faithfully and fruitfully. Many times in the journey of life, we find ourselves thinking or saying "How I wish I had known that back when." It is the author's hope that this book will help some Christians to have at least fewer such moments.

*So You Want to Follow Jesus?* is an "overview" of the journey of discipleship. It is a distillation of personal observations from a lifetime of ministry and commonsense conclusions about living for Christ. Discipleship begins in the heart and continues in the heart, but that "burning heart" will set all of life aglow and become a contagious witness. The Jesus who saves must become Lord of our lives so that He may become Savior and Lord of other's lives. That is *following Jesus* in the third millennium or any other millennium.

Elton Trueblood wrote of the mid-twentieth century culture something that is still true of our culture today. He said, "we do not expect, for the most part, to find the gospel centered in a burning conviction which will make men and women change occupations, go to the end of the earth, alter the practices of governments, redirect culture, and remake civilization . . . we welcome religion, but we expect it to be innocuous, and above all, unfanatical. We are willing to accept it, provided that it involves no zeal."[5] Yet this is precisely what following Jesus in genuine discipleship has involved throughout history.

Trueblood said, "The minimum conditions of membership in the nameless order of the Church universal are five: *commitment, witness, fellowship, vocation*, and *discipline*."[6] I have attempted to address each of these in *So You Want to Follow Jesus?*

Ron Sider writes: "You and I will face breathtaking possibilities and deadly dangers in the next millennium. It could be hell. Or it could be Christianity's finest hour. Jesus' goal and his strategy will continue the same . . . Jesus' plan is to win the world through His followers—you and me, and He has no back-up plan."[7]

Judson Jerome, well-known poet and literary critic has counseled would-be writers this way: "if you don't feel that it is terribly important that many people read this now . . . I wish you would not clutter the mail. Our civilization has very little time, and it is important that we weed out our messages and state the essential ones carefully."[8] This author believes that *So You Want to Follow Jesus?* is an essential message for our times.

# CHAPTER ONE

# HAVE I ANSWERED MY CALL FROM JESUS?

*It is possible to be grossly selfish in absorbing the salvation of Jesus, to enjoy all its benedictions, and never follow Him one step.*

—Oswald Chambers

*Abstract or unembodied Christianity is a fiction.*

—Elton Trueblood

There's a little game my wife and I play when we are at home, relaxed in our easy chairs, reading the evening paper, a good book, or perhaps watching television. When the phone rings, we both wonder who's going to make the first move toward answering the call, and so we each try to "outslow" the other. Despite a normal amount of curiosity about the as-yet-unknown caller, there is nevertheless a certain amount of hesitancy about being disturbed out of our relaxed condition and comfort.

So, for a couple of rings or so, neither of us makes a move. We may steal a glance at one another with that questioning look on our faces—"are you going to get this one?" When the call is from one of our children or from some otherwise interesting caller rather than another "long-distance carrier," or other telemarketing scheme, the one who played the tune, "I Shall Not Be Moved" the longest now wishes he or she had answered that call.

## God Is Seeking a Relationship with Me

There is a sense in which Jesus is always "ringing my number" in order to kindly, but insistently deliver His invitation: "Follow Me." It's the most important call I, or anyone will ever get. I cannot afford to play games with this call, and no one else can answer it for me. I may put Jesus on "hold," or "call waiting," but no matter how often I try to avoid the call, He still is ringing my number (Rev. 3:20). Even if I try to "screen" the calls, my "caller ID" will let me know that *it is Jesus still trying to get through.*

From the beginning of time, God has been personally involved in seeking to establish a relationship with all persons. In the Garden of Eden, after the first man and woman had ignored God's clear command, and had sneaked away in shame, the "seeking God" came to them calling, "Where are you?" (Gen. 3:9). And, from the beginning of *my* time and *your* time, God has taken the initiative in seeking a relationship with you and me.

Jesus defined His own mission succinctly: "For the Son of Man came to seek and to save that which was lost" (Lk. 19:10). And each of the three stories that Jesus told, as related in Luke 15, reveal to us a God who loves each person and is searching for them like the woman who lost the silver coin, like the shepherd who seeks the lost sheep, and like the father who patiently waits for the prodigal son to come home, yet runs to meet him with an offer of forgiveness.

The loneliness that I feel, the ultimate insecurity that gnaws at my soul, and those nagging questions that won't go away—questions like, "Who am I?" "Where Did I come From?" "Why am I here?" "What's wrong with my life?" "What can fix my life?" These very questions are all evidences that God is searching for me. *It is Jesus ringing my number.*

The real question for me is "Have *I* responded to His call? You see, the gospel makes individuals out of everyone of us. Oswald Chambers reminds us, "Whenever our Lord speaks of discipleship He prefaces what He says with an 'if.' Discipleship must always be a *personal* matter; we can never become disciples in crowds, or even in two's . . ."[1] And Dietrich Bonhoeffer writes: "Every man is called separately, and must follow alone."[2] No one can answer my call to follow Jesus but me.

As Dave Breese says, "*I am the object of divine initiative . . .* God has taken every step possible to come to me where I am in order that I may ultimately go to be with Him where He is."[3]

## Why Am I Delaying My Response?

If I am putting off answering my personal call from Jesus, there is a reason. Bonhoeffer put it this way: "Somewhere in your heart you are refusing to listen to His call. *Your difficulty is your sins. . . .* No one should be surprised," writes Bonhoeffer, "at the difficulty of faith if there is some part of his life where he is consciously resisting or disobeying the commandment of Jesus. Is there some part of your life which you are refusing to surrender . . . some sinful passion, maybe, or some animosity, some hope, perhaps your ambition, or your reason. If so, you must not be surprised that you have not received the Holy Spirit, that prayer is difficult, or that your request for faith remains unanswered."[4]

J. Heinrich Arnold says, "You need to become absolutely determined to follow Jesus. It is not true that you are too weak to overcome sin—that is a lie of the devil. In Jesus *it is possible to overcome sin. That is why he died on the cross.* Live totally for him."[5]

Oswald Chambers puts it even more strongly perhaps: "if you really were sick of yourself you would go to your own funeral and forever after let God be all in all. Until you get to that point you will never have faith in God."[6]

What is there in my life I am unwilling to give up for Jesus? Again, Bonhoeffer pleads, "Tear yourself away from all other attachments, and follow him . . . without this preliminary step of obedience, our faith will only be pious humbug, and lead us to the grace which is not costly."[7]

George Buttrick writes: "Charge Christ with presumption or egomania, the fact stands. Christ presented his claims, and then brooked no argument: the person called said 'yes' or 'no.'"[8] Christ is calling *me*. Is my answer *yes* or *no*?

## Have I Experienced the "New Birth"?

Although this is a book about *discipleship*, and not the "new birth," or the experience of grace that we call salvation, for most persons the first step in following Jesus begins with what Jesus calls being "born again." "I tell you the truth," said Jesus, "No one can see the kingdom of God, unless he is born again" (Jn. 3:3). Perhaps I might wish to think of this experience as the "Start-up Disk" for God's program of discipleship in my life. God provides the "software," but I've got to choose to install it in my own personal life.

Upon honest inquiry, Nicodemus learned that this new birth was not a fleshly (physical) birth, but a *spiritual* birth. Jesus said, "Flesh gives birth to flesh, but the Spirit gives birth to spirit" (Jn. 3:6). What happens by the Spirit then? Bible scholars agree that this "new birth" is the result of personal repentance and faith. Repentance, the sincere and godly sorrow for one's sins, and a willingness to turn from them, enables one to place his or her personal trust in Christ, whose sacrificial death atones for those sins. New *spiritual* life is generated within the individual heart and life.

The new birth, then, is a spiritual change wrought in the heart of a repentant sinner by *faith*. "For it is by grace you have been saved, through faith—and this is not from yourselves, it is the gift of God—not by works so that no one can boast" (Eph. 2:8,9). Our salvation is not obtained by "good works," but by *faith.*

A computer has what's called "an operating system"—the software that runs the computer. The question I must face is: "Whose *software* is running my life—God's or Satan's?" Faith in Christ is God's way of "booting-up" my spiritual life and beginning the journey of discipleship.

Have I taken the first step in following Jesus? Have *I* repented of my sins? Have I been *born again,* as Jesus says I must? Taking the first step in following Jesus turns faith into obedience and begins the "long obedience of discipleship." Bonhoeffer writes, "The road to faith passes through obedience to the call of Jesus. Unless a definite step is demanded the call vanishes into thin air, and if men imagine that they can follow Jesus without taking this step, they are deluding themselves like fanatics."[9]

## Have I Been Obedient in Baptism?

Having responded to the call of Jesus by leaving all to follow Him, one of the first glad steps of obedience is that of *baptism.* Jesus said, "If anyone is ashamed of me and my words in this adulterous generation, the Son of Man will be ashamed of him when he comes in his Father's glory with the holy angels" (Mk. 8:38). Shortly before His ascension, Jesus issued instructions to His followers to go and make disciples, "*baptizing* them in the name of the Father and of the Son and of the Holy Spirit, and teaching them to obey everything I have commanded you" (Mt. 28:19, emphasis mine).

Church historian, Bruce Shelly says that the first Christians "inaugurated a new age and people could enter life in that spiritual kingdom by faith in Jesus as Lord and *witness to that faith by baptism.*"[10]

It is clearly the will and command of the Lord that all His followers should be baptized. Answering the incredulity of Nicodemus, when Jesus declared that a man must be born again, Jesus explained further: "I tell you the truth, no one can enter the kingdom of God unless he is born of *water* and the *Spirit*" (Jn. 3:5).

John Wesley interpreted these words to mean: "Except he experience that great inward change by the Spirit and be baptized (whenever baptism can be had) as the outward sign and means of it."[11] Theologian, H. Orton Wiley, also believed the water to refer to baptism, saying "Here, evidently, the sign is the outward baptism with water, and the thing signified is the inner work of the Spirit."[12]

Rob Staples writes: "From Genesis to Revelation, and everywhere in between, God marked His people." Baptism, among other things is to bear the mark of Christ's name and nature. As Staples says, we are "incarnations of God's love in the world! Persons marked with Christ's name."[13] Isn't that beautiful? Am I one of the "marked ones"?

Staples says, "Baptism, as it is known in the New Testament and practiced in the Church, is the first of two sacraments recognized by Protestants. It is administered only once, at the point of initiation into the Christian community. The forms and modes of administration vary greatly . . . but the essential action and accompanying words are quite uniform and consistent."[14] The other sacrament, of course, is the Lord's Supper. We do not concern ourselves with that sacrament here.

Repentance and faith should *precede* the Christian rite of baptism. On the day of Pentecost, Peter urged his listeners to "repent and be baptized, everyone of you, in the name of Jesus Christ for the forgiveness of your sins (Acts 2:38).

To be baptized in the Christian faith is to be identified with Christ in His death and His resurrection. The Apostle Paul, in his letter to the Roman converts, wrote: "What shall we say, then? Shall we go on sinning so that grace may increase? By no means! We died to sin; how can we live in it any longer? Or don't you know that all of us who were baptized into Christ Jesus were baptized into His death?

We were buried with Him through baptism into death in order that, just as Christ was raised from the dead through the glory of the Father, we too may live a new life" (Rom. 6:1–4).

In other words, baptism is to be a beautiful symbolic dramatization of the disciple's death to sin in his own life, and the beginning of a new life of faith and obedience through the power of the resurrection. It is important to understand that *baptism is not something we do in order to be saved*, but an act of obedience in response to Christ's forgiving love and His command. Baptism is an outward symbol of an inward work of grace.

## Getting off the Blocks Is Just the Beginning

The new birth and baptism are like twin starting blocks in launching one into the Christian race. A race always has "starting blocks" and a "finish line," but one cannot cross that finish line without taking that first step—without getting "off the blocks." Following Jesus is a "journey," not just a step. It is a race—a marathon race, *not a sprint*.

The 240,000 mile journey to the moon for Neil Armstrong and his fellow astronauts began with a *launch*, but it led to a safe landing on the lunar surface where Armstrong immortalized those words, "One small step for man—one giant leap for mankind." The journey with Jesus begins with the first step, but it will be one giant leap forward in your life and ultimately can result in a safe landing in heaven.

The question for me today is: Have I taken that first step? Have I begun the journey? Mother Teresa said, "With a will that is whole I will love God, I will opt for Him, I will run toward Him, I will reach Him, I will possess Him."[15] That is the kind of determination it takes to enter the race and finish the race.

Answering the call to follow Jesus in serious discipleship is the best decision one will ever make. As Blackaby writes: "As you respond to Him in simple childlike trust, you will find a whole new way of looking at life begin to unfold for you. Your life will be fulfilling. You will never have a sense of emptiness or a lack of purpose. He always fills your life with Himself. When you have Him, you have everything there is. As He was to Moses, He will be to you, the 'I Am That I Am.'"[16]

Again, Mother Teresa says, "you must not be afraid to say 'yes' to Jesus, because there is no greater love than His love and no greater joy than His joy. My prayer for you is that you come to understand and have the courage to answer Jesus' call to you with the simple word, 'Yes.'"[17]

## Discipleship Does Not Make One a Christian

Lewis Smedes, in his book *Mere Morality* builds a strong case for the necessity of a basic morality to hold society together. Nevertheless, he cautions that "mere morality does not make anyone a Christian,"[18] Only grace through faith does that. "For in the gospel a righteousness from God is revealed, a righteousness that is by faith from first to last, just as it is written: 'The righteous will live by faith'" (Rom. 1:17).

So also, it should be said up front that "mere discipleship" does not make anyone a Christian. Only Christ can do that through the new birth, but a reasonable person knows that discipleship—*following Jesus*—should follow sincere faith and the new-birth experience.

If one believes that Jesus has the power to forgive sins and to grant eternal life, and trusts Him for that initial experience of grace, it is only reasonable to expect that Jesus has a claim upon the whole of his or her life, and has a right to say, "follow me everyday, in every way, and *all the way*."

"And if we answer the call to discipleship, where will it lead us," asks Bonhoeffer, and adds, "Only Jesus Christ, who bids us follow him, knows the journey's end. But we do know that it will be a road of boundless mercy."[19] As Dave Breese says, "though you may have received Christ with the smallest flicker of faith, you have begun a life that shall be vindicated in the flaming reality of eternity. Having begun with Christ, now take the next step."[20]

So I have now answered His call. I have decided to follow Jesus, but perhaps it would be wise to carefully consider what it is that Jesus calls us to. What will answering His call mean to my life personally? In the next chapter we will ponder the cost, dimensions, and full implications of discipleship—of following Jesus.

## QUESTIONS FOR REFLECTION

1. What specific steps of obedience and response to Jesus' call can I identify in my own life?

2. If I have not responded to His call, can I be honest about *why* I am delaying my response to Jesus call?

3. Is there an experience in my life that I can identify as a "new birth" experience? Describe it.

4. Could I describe that experience as the "Start-up Disk" for God's plan of discipleship in my life?

5. Have I allowed Christ to "mark" me as one of His disciples through the sacrament of water baptism? Explain what that experience has meant to you.

6. What should *precede* the Christian rite of baptism?

7. What does the author mean by "getting off the blocks"?

8. Does discipleship make one a Christian. Explain the difference.

## A PRAYER FOR SERIOUS FOLLOWERS

Jesus, I know I have been the object of divine initiative. You have knocked at my door. You have rung my number, and personally invited me to follow You.

I open the door of my heart and life to you through repentance and faith. I receive your mercy and grace. I receive YOU, and I gladly receive the sacrament of Christian baptism, and rejoice to be one of your "marked" ones.

Jesus, I know that I have just gotten "off the blocks" in my journey of discipleship, but my "yes" to you is not just for today, but for *every* day, and for *forever*. Amen.

# CHAPTER TWO

# WHAT IS THE CALL TO DISCIPLESHIP, ANYWAY?

*The call of God embarrasses us because of two things—it presents us with sealed orders, and urges us to a vast venture.*
—Oswald Chambers

*Since Christianity has never survived on the basis of mild and uncommitted theism, it is certainly not likely to survive on that basis today.*
—Elton Trueblood

Jesus didn't just call His followers to *believe* in Him, or to receive and wallow in His love and forgiveness. Nor did He just have in mind their fondling of an intimate personal relationship with Him, as precious as that relationship is. Jesus calls every believer and follower to serious discipleship.

"To Call" according to the dictionary, is to speak in a distinct voice so as to be heard. It is to make a request or demand, to summon to a particular activity—such as a call to duty or to service. A "call" can also mean "to rouse from sleep—to awaken." That is what this author hopes will happen to believers, or unbelievers, who read this book.

Are you intrigued by the idea of *discipleship*? I am. No doubt that's why I am writing this book. But it is more than a personal preference or interest. Discipleship is a vital New Testament phenomenon with serious implications for all Christians, and indeed for our world.

The word *disciple* occurs 269 times in the New Testament, while the word *Christian* is found only three times. Dallas Willard says, "The New Testament is a book *about* disciples, *by* disciples and *for* disciples of Jesus Christ."[1] The word *disciple* in the Greek means simply "pupil" or "learner." In the New Testament, the term applies to both Jesus' original twelve apostles, whom He called and appointed, and also to *all* of His followers.

Greg Laurie writes, "It is my conviction that every disciple is a believer, but not every believer is a disciple."[2] Is it possible then to be a Christian without being a disciple? This book, you will find, gets to the heart of that question and its answer.

Question: *Why has Christianity failed to impact and transform the culture and the power structures of this world*? Dallas Willard writes: "By modest estimate, more than a quarter of the entire population of the United States have professed an evangelical conversion experience." Willard then quotes William Iverson who observes that "a pound of meat would surely be affected by a quarter pound of salt. If this is real Christianity, the 'salt of the earth,' where is the effect of which Jesus spoke?"[3]

And Ron Sider pointedly asks, "What would it take to change this world for the better?" And the response to his own question was: "It would take just a tiny fraction of today's Christians truly believing what Jesus taught and living the way Jesus lived."[4] Isn't that what discipleship is all about?

Keith Phillips says, "Jesus came to save a fallen race and raise up a people who would praise Him forever. In the discharge of this mission, He ministered among us as a servant, caring for the sick, healing the brokenhearted, and preaching the gospel to the multitudes. But through it all He concentrated His attention upon the *making of disciples*—persons who would learn of Him and follow in His steps."[5]

Sider exposes at least part of the reason why Christianity without discipleship has been so popular. He says, "Jesus insisted that discipleship is impossible without self-denial. Instant gratification is at the core of modern life. Costly self-denial is at the center of Jesus' way."[6] Will we take the "cross," or the soft cushion?

Sider says, "The very thought of self-denial grates on modern hearts. They prefer the quick fix delusion of instant gratification. That attitude is behind our runaway divorce rates and abortion on demand—it is too tough and costly to learn mutual submission in marriage and care for inconvenient, unexpected babies."[7]

## Discipleship Begins with Faith

As we observed in Chapter One, discipleship begins with a personal faith in Jesus Christ. From that faith the genesis of a new humanity springs forth, but the new humanity is developed on an individual basis. Jesus calls us one by one, and through God's grace, one by one we are enabled to practice the discipline of discipleship and grow into mature believers, bearing the love, wisdom, and power of God throughout human society.

"True discipleship," says Greg Laurie, "is getting back to the Christian life as it was meant to be lived. In one sense we might call it *radical Christian living*. When we compare it to the anemic substitute people often offer as the Christian life today, it most certainly is radical . . . we must embrace discipleship just as Christ offered it, the disciples apprehended it, and the early church lived it!"[8]

## Discipleship Is the Call to Follow-ship

Perhaps there is no better definition of Christian discipleship than simply *following Jesus*. The Bible says, "As He (Jesus) walked along, he saw Levi, son of Alphaeus sitting at a tax collector's booth. 'Follow me' Jesus told him, and Levi got up and followed him" (Mk. 2:14).

Discipleship today and in the new millennium begins just where it has always begun—with a personal response to the call of Jesus— "come, follow me." Jesus' calling of His first disciples serves as a pattern, or a "divine template" of the call that He places upon the hearts and lives of people in every generation. Jesus is still calling people to follow Him—to become pupils and learners at His feet. But what does it mean to answer that call?

We know what it meant to the followers of Jesus in the First Century to follow Jesus, but do we have any modern examples? What follows here is just one example of true and radical discipleship from the mid-twentieth century.

## An Example of True Discipleship and Followship

The world was shocked in January of 1956 by the story of five young missionary men who were speared to death in the Equadorian jungle. The men were trying to take the gospel and the love of Christ to the primitive Auca Indian tribe.

Although fully aware that the Aucas were known for their fierce tribal infighting and their hatred of "outsiders," the missionaries had vowed to each other before God that they would not defend themselves if attacked, even in the face of death.

What would cause Nate Saint, Jim Elliot, Roger Youderian, Ed McCully, and Peter Fleming to willingly lay downs their lives in such noble sacrifice? And what would cause the widow of Jim Elliot and the sister of Nate Saint to take the baton handed off by their murdered loved ones, and within three years, to be actually living among the Aucas, practicing basic medicine, learning the language, and sharing the story of Jesus?

A peek into that tribal culture today, some forty years later, would demonstrate the power of Christ's love to break down barriers. For example one would find Steve Saint, Nate's son, sitting around a campfire with six of the very Aucas who participated in the killing of his father and the other four missionaries. You would hear the Aucas provide the details of how the killings took place. They could do this without fear of retaliation for they had all experienced the power of forgiveness and reconciliation. They had all heard the call of Jesus to serious followship, and had courageously answered that call.

There are many other examples. The pages of history are stained with the blood of Jesus' disciples. Answering *my* call to discipleship may not mean literal martyrdom, but if I am serious about following Jesus, I must understand what it does require—what the call to discipleship means.

## Discipleship Is a Call to a Relationship of Love

The call to follow Jesus is first of all a call *to adjust one's love life.* When Jesus was asked what was the greatest commandment of all, He responded, saying, "Love the Lord your God with all your heart and with all your soul and with all your mind. This is the first and greatest commandment. And the second is like it; Love your neighbor as yourself. All the Law and the Prophets hang on these two commandments" (Mk. 22:37–40).

The call to follow Jesus is a call to a *relationship*—a relationship of love. God desires that above all. Henry Blackaby, in his popular book, *Experiencing God,* writes: "More than anything else that you might do, *God wants you to love Him with your total being. He created you for that purpose. If your love relationship is out of line, everything else related to knowing, doing, and experiencing God's will will be messed up.*"[9]

Love, of course, is built on "trust" and so the call to follow Jesus is also a call to *trust*. It is a call to a *personal trust in the person of the Savior*. A trust that He really is who He said He was—The Way, the Truth, and the Life. A trust that Jesus is not only the Savior and Redeemer of the world, but that He is *my* Savior.. A trust that He has a better plan for my life.

## Discipleship Is a Call to Obedience

Dietrich Bonhoeffer, reflecting upon Levi's immediate response to the call of Jesus asks, "And what does the text inform us about the content of discipleship?" He answers his own question, saying, "*Follow me, run along behind me! That is all.*" [10]

Surely Bonhoeffer succinctly cuts through to the heart of discipleship here, but it needs a bit of explanation. Perhaps what he meant by the "content" of discipleship has more to do with the "cost" of discipleship. At least that is the title of his classic work, *The Cost of Discipleship*, and that may very well expose the "core" of genuine discipleship.

Bonhoeffer allows no easy-believism, devoid of reformation of life and concrete obedience. Blackaby writes, "Obedience is our moment of truth. It reveals what I really believe about God, whether I will experience His mighty work in and through me, and whether I will come to know Him even more intimately."[11]

When called by Jesus, Peter and John left their nets and boats (major adjustment), and followed Him (obedience). This is faith translated into action—belief emerging as *changed lifestyle*. E. Stanley Jones once wrote: "The word *belief* really means *by-lief*, by life. The only creed you believe is the creed you act upon *by-lief*, by life."[12]

J. Heinrich Arnold says, "Discipleship means complete dedication. It demands everything—the whole heart, the whole mind, and the whole life, including one's time, energy, and property—for the cause of love. Half-hearted Christianity is worse than no Christianity."[13]

## Discipleship Is Following Without Seeing the End

Centuries before the New Testament disciples, a man named Abram (later called Abraham), had been called by God to leave the familiarity and security of his family and homeland "to go out to the land I will show you" (Gen. 12:1). Henry Blackaby asks, "Does God call people to follow Him without giving them all the details up front?" He answers: "Many times, as with Abram, God called people just to follow Him. He is more likely to call you to follow one day at a time than He is to spell out all the details before you begin to obey Him."[14]

Oswald Chambers writes, "When Jesus Christ says 'Follow Me,' He never says to where. The consequences must be left entirely to Him . . . we have to stand true to the fact of God's call and smilingly wash our hands of the consequences."[15]

And, Bonhoeffer, writing of Levi's response, says, "the old life is left behind and completely surrendered. The disciple is dragged out of his relative security into a life of absolute insecurity (that is in truth into the absolute security and safety of the fellowship of Jesus)."[16]

Jesus will allow no competing loyalties—not even from one's family. Like "Christian" in *Pilgrim's Progress*," the follower of Jesus must put his fingers in his ears and run on crying, "Life! Life! Eternal Life."[17]

John White, speaking of the cost of discipleship, writes: "We will have to place on the table career, money, affection, ambition, plans, hobbies, and our very lives, and say, 'It hurts me to place these here, but I know you can replace them a hundredfold. Let them be disposed of as they may—returned to me or lost forever. Their fate will not influence my choice. I want to follow you wholly."[18]

Or as Michael Molinos, the seventeenth-century mystic, says, "We find Him only where *He* is *all* and where we are nothing."[19]

## Following Jesus Is Not an Experiment

Following Jesus is a revolutionary change in one's thinking and in one's lifestyle, and it requires a commitment that brooks no retreat. It is said that Phillip of Macedonia, father of Alexander the Great, once had the ladders used by his soldiers when storming a walled city, removed from behind them *so that they could not give up or retreat.* They had to conquer or die. Likewise there is a story out of the Crusades, where, in an invasion by sea, the soldiers were commanded to burn their boats so there would be no possibility of leaving the scene of battle.

"Boats and ladders—what are they," asked Amy Carmichael, the famous missionary to India? She answered her readers, "they are ways of retreat from difficult things, from fights with the great enemy of souls," and she asked even more directly, "have we any boats unburned? Any ladders not flung down?"[20]

Following Jesus requires that we tear ourselves away from all other attachments. "It is nothing else," writes Bonhoeffer, "than bondage to Jesus Christ alone, complete breaking through every program, every ideal, every set of laws. No other significance is possible, since Jesus is the only significance. *Beside Jesus nothing has any significance. He alone matters.*"[21]

## Why Do People Respond to Jesus' Call?

Returning to the original "tintype"—to that simple call to Levi, we might curiously wonder, what caused his immediate response? Bonhoeffer says the Bible shows no interest whatsoever in the psychological reasons behind Levi's response to the call of Jesus. He writes simply, "It is Jesus who calls, and because it is Jesus, Levi follows at once. This encounter is a testimony to the absolute, direct, and unaccountable authority of Jesus."[22]

We need not read "unconditional predestination" here. It is not as though Simon Peter or John, or Levi had no choice upon hearing the call of Jesus. It is, however, a divine-human encounter that lifts it above all other encounters. *They came face to face with Jesus—the Son of God.*

Oswald Chambers says, "When once the face of the Lord Jesus Christ has broken through, all ecstasies and experiences dwindle in His presence, and the one dominant leadership becomes more and more clear. We have seen Jesus as we never saw Him before, and the impulsion in us by the grace of God is that *we must follow in His steps.*"[23]

Henry Blackaby says, "God takes the initiative. When He comes to a person, He always reveals Himself and His activity. That revelation is always an invitation for the individual to adjust his life to God."[24] It is a call to get involved in what God is doing in this world.

## Will Third-Millennium Persons Respond to His Call?

One may wonder, "Are people still responding to the invitation of this first-century Galilean Fisherman?" Today, when the Eastern religions exercise new influence, and the Muslim religion is rapidly exploding even in America, will people still respond to the call of Jesus?

Given the attractions of a high-tech, cyberspace world with its fascinations and promise of prosperity, and considering the collapse of morals in the culture, the unraveling of the fabric of the family, and the apparent impotence of the church to impact our culture (at least in the Western world), one cannot be faulted for asking, "Who will respond to the call of Jesus in the first century of the third millennium?"

Read that, "Will anyone respond?"

To answer that question, one only has to take a cursory look at twenty centuries of history. From the very first call of Jesus to Simon and Andrew to the present moment, the words, "Follow

Me" have found a mystical authority and resonance in the hearts of multitudes.

Even in the darkest moments of history, whether in the hostile days of Nero, the Dark Ages, or the Reformation days of Martin Luther, when he bravely posted his 95 theses on the door at Wittenberg, the voice of God has been heard and responded to with glad obedience—even when that obedience meant being burned at a stake.

Is there any reason to believe that those divinely-charged, simple words, "Follow Me" will lose their invitational charm or fail to cast their holy spell in the new millennium? As Douglas Groothuis reminds us, "The mightiest hard drive, the fastest modem, the most sophisticated word processor, and the most powerful internet search engines on the planet will not download wisdom into the human soul."[25] Nor can they download salvation or necessarily develop the soul.

God is a "speaking" God. "In the past, God spoke to our fore-fathers through the prophets at many times and in various ways, but in these last days he has spoken to us by his Son, whom he appointed heir of all things, and through whom he made the uni-verse. The Son is the radiance of God's glory and the exact repre-sentation of his being, sustaining all things by his powerful word" (Heb. 1:1–3).

It is the Son's voice we hear today. He is saying, "Follow Me." It is a powerful word, calling for a compete commitment. Now that I have answered that call and carefully considered its full implica-tions, what kind of follower will *I* be?

# QUESTIONS FOR REFLECTION

1.  Have I read, or "read again" the Gospel accounts of Jesus' calling of His first disciples?

2.  What evidence do I see in the world that Jesus is still calling men to follow Him?

3.  What evidence do I see in my own personal life and world that Jesus is calling *me* to discipleship?

4.  What is discipleship a call to?

5.  What are the things in my life that might keep me from "forsaking all" to follow Jesus?

6.  In what way is "following Jesus," not an *experiment*? Do I have any "boats" tied up and waiting, or any "ladders" ready for retreat?

7.  Discuss what Bonhoeffer meant when he said, "apart from Jesus, nothing has any significance." Do you agree?

8.  Am I willing to immerse myself in the Gospels (the history of Christ's ministry *to* and *through* His disciples)?

## A PRAYER FOR SERIOUS FOLLOWERS

Jesus, your Word and yesterday's disciples and martyrs teach me clearly what answering your call will mean. Help me not to shrink from that reality, but to freely and gladly embrace the cross.

I want you to "burn my boats and fling down my ladders," for I know that apart from you, nothing has any significance. You alone matter. I will be your disciple. Let me be an eager learner at your feet, and let me faithfully follow You, regardless of the cost. In Your name. Amen.

# CHAPTER THREE

# AM I WILLING TO FOLLOW JESUS WHOLEHEARTEDLY?

*Those of us who have entered into a conscious experience of the salvation of Jesus by the Grace of God, whose whole inner life is drawn toward God, have the privilege of being disciples if we will.*

—Oswald Chambers

*One Treasure, a single eye, and a sole Master.*

—Jim Elliot

There is a difference between being saved and being a disciple, says Oswald Chambers. "We are grateful to God for saving us from sin, but we are of no use to Him in so far as our actual life is concerned. We are not spiritual disciples . . . we cannot make disciples of others unless we are disciples ourselves."[1]

Dallas Willard asks an extremely important question: "How can ordinary human beings such as you and I—who must live in circumstances all too commonplace—follow and become like Jesus Christ? How can we be like Christ always—not just on Sundays when we're on our best behavior, surrounded by others to cheer and sustain us?"[2] Perhaps there is not a simple answer to that, but God does not leave us without "guideposts."

When I've answered the call to follow Jesus, I've only taken a "first" step. I must now decide what kind of follower I will be. Will I, like Caleb, follow the Lord wholeheartedly? (Josh. 14:8,9).

That there are vast differences in Christians or those who profess to follow Christ is clearly obvious, but why do some people seem to know God better than others? Why do the lives of some of Christ's followers have a greater impact and influence upon the world or upon the community of believers than other lives?

What accounts for the differences in Christians? Surely God has no "favorites." Surely it is not just differences in temperaments or personalities, though that influence cannot be denied or excluded.

The great saints of Biblical and post-Biblical times vary greatly in temperament, personality, social status, education, and background, yet they all had intimate relationships with God and impacted their culture dramatically. What accounts for that? Ultimately, the differences are not with God, but with the individual.

## Spiritual Receptivity and Responsiveness

A. W. Tozer believed that these great souls all had in common *spiritual receptivity*. He writes: "Something in them was open to heaven, something which urged them Godward . . . I shall say simply that they had spiritual awareness and that they went on to cultivate it until it became the biggest thing in their lives. They differed," said Tozer, "in that when they felt the inward longing *they did something about it*. They acquired the lifelong habit of spiritual response."[3]

Certainly this "spiritual sensitivity" or responsiveness to God—His way, His Word, His will—can be cultivated or neglected. Again, Tozer claims, "the idea of cultivation and exercise so dear to the saints of old, has now no place in our total religious picture. It is too slow, too common. We now demand glamor and fast flowing dramatic action."[4]

One can imagine what Tozer would write about life today. Generations reared amid the automation, high-tech and cyberspace developments of this instant information age are experiencing difficulty learning how to develop the soul. Douglas Groothuis writes, "Without times of reflection, meditations, prayer, silence, and solitude—unplugged and unwired moments—we lack the interior resources to govern our tongues, keyboards, and screens so that our words and lives will edify those around us and honor our Creator."

Of his own times, Tozer warned, "It will require a determined heart and more than a little courage to wrench ourselves loose from the grip of our times and return to biblical ways."[6]

## The Disciple Must Be Disentangled

Did you ever pick blackberries? If you did, you learned about both entanglement and disentanglement almost instantly. I'm sure you discovered also that it is much easier to get entangled than it is to get disentangled.

Reaching for that luscious-looking berry, you suddenly found yourself "snagged" on all sides at once. Becoming unsnagged was your chief occupation for the next five minutes while you worriedly watched berry after berry thumping into your partner's bucket.

Once should be enough. The problem is, those "luscious-lookers" keep popping up everywhere. Time and time again you find yourself suckered into the snags. Getting unsnagged is never easy, and often not without pain, but it is the only way to be free and fruitful. The disciple, too, must be disentangled if he or she is to be *free* and *fruitful* in the Lord. From what, then, must I be disentangled?

*I must give up sin.* In his *Approved Unto God*, Oswald Chambers says, "A disciple of Jesus must know from what to be disentangled."[7] It ought to be clear to any serious student of the Bible that the disciple must be disentangled from *sin*. Nothing will so tangle, threaten, and snag one's spiritual life and growth as known sin or disobedience.

To the Corinthians, some of whom were professing to follow Christ while allowing shameful and sinful practices in their lives, Paul spoke sternly: "Come back to your senses as you ought, and stop sinning" (1 Cor. 15:34), or as Kenneth Taylor translates it, "Get some sense, and quit your sinning" (TLB).

In Romans, the Apostle deals in the graphic imagery of life and death. Anticipating a satanic trap for the disciples, Paul asks, "What shall we say, then? Shall we go on sinning so that grace may increase? By no means! We died to sin; how can we live in it any longer? (Rom. 6:1,2). He warns them this way: "For we know that our old self was crucified with him (Christ) so that the body of sin might be done away with, that we should no longer be slaves to sin—because anyone who has died has been freed from sin" (Rom. 6:6,7).

Nowhere in the Bible is disentanglement from sin taught more forcibly than by Jesus in the Sermon on the Mount. Jesus taught a radical dealing not only with *sins*, but also with the very spring of *sinfulness*. He went beyond the deed to the disposition.

Dr. E. Stanley Jones wrote that our "present day" Christianity is anemic and weak, and "needs a blood transfusion from the Sermon on the Mount."[8]

***I must be willing to give up even legitimate things***. Discipleship requires sin to go, but if one thinks that sin is the only thing to give up to be a serious follower of Jesus, he or she is widely missing the mark. The thrust of discipleship goes much deeper. Chambers says that Paul argues this way in 1 Cor. 8:13, "If anything in me, right or wrong, is hindering God's work and causing another to stumble, I will give it up, even if it is the most legitimate thing on earth."[9]

There are many otherwise "good" and "legitimate" things that will be laid aside because of the singular devotion of the disciple. The writer to the Hebrews, using the image of the runner, says the disciple must strip down and discard anything that hinders his or her running. Anything that would bog one down, restrict growth, or retard God's work in and through the disciple must be tossed aside.

Comparing the disciple to a soldier, Paul says, "No one serving as a soldier gets involved in civilian affairs—he wants to please his commanding officer" (2 Tim. 2:4). "Civilian affairs" here would not necessarily be "wrong" or "evil" affairs. They would likely just be secular affairs that occupy too much time or that receive improper priority. Jesus spoke of the "cares of this world" choking out our fruitfulness (Mk. 4:19).

Again, Oswald Chambers says, "If we are willing to give up *wrong* things only for Jesus Christ, never let us talk about being in love with Him."[10] Upon reading in God's Word, "He makes His ministers a flame of fire," Jim Elliot wrote, "Am I ignitable? God deliver me from the dread asbestos of 'other things.' Saturate me with the oil of the Spirit, that I may be aflame."[11]

The disciple of Jesus must disentangle himself from the "civies" of many ordinary and legitimate things in order to serve Him who called him or her to spiritual soldiering. The disciple wants to please the Commander-in-Chief.

## Jesus Calls to an Exclusionary Love

Many today make discipleship easy. Jesus never did. The call to follow Him was always costly. Bruce Shelley says "Jesus made a persistent point about a special kind of life that separated the 'kingdom of God' from rival authorities among men. Little by little his disciples came to see that following him meant saying 'no' to other voices calling for their loyalties."[12]

The disentanglement Jesus required involved a radical, "exclusionary love." He said, "If anyone comes to me and does not hate his father and mother, his wife and children, his brothers and sisters—yes, even his own life—he cannot be my disciple" (Lk. 14:26).

Jesus was not counseling carnal malice or ill treatment for one's family, but He knew that strong familial relationships would become a serious competitor for the place of supreme love and devotion deserved only by Him.

The most radical and important statement of the New Testament regarding discipleship may very well be Jesus' words, "any of you who does not give up everything he has cannot be my disciple" (Lk. 14:33). That is divine disentanglement and discipleship in a nutshell.

## We Are Not Museum Pieces

A final word of caution may be necessary though. Disentanglement must not lead to a "spiritual monasticism." The disciple is not intended to become a museum piece even for self-development purposes.

Oswald Chambers reminds us, "We are not here to develop our own spiritual life, but to be broken for Jesus Christ's sake. . . . If you want to remain a full-orbed grape, you must keep out of God's hands, for He will crush you, wine cannot be had any other way."[13]

Jim Elliot penned into his journal the following words, upon reading Amy Carmichael's *Gold Cord*, and her words:

"No wound? No scar?
Yet as the Master shall the servant be,
And pierced are the feet that follow me:
But thine are whole: Can he have followed far
Who has no wound, nor scar?"

"How can I write the effect it has upon me?" wrote Jim, "Ah what a sham I am carrying on in the name of spirituality! No scar? No scar. No tear? No tear. But I hear you talk so well! Yes, I talk well. O God of the thorny crown, please, in Thy tender mercy, privilege me to walk thy path of royalty." (God answered his prayer six years later—allowing Jim to become a martyr for Christ.)

He continued, "I do not understand why I have never seen in America what missionaries write of—that sense of swords being drawn, the smell of war with demon powers . . . as a result, our warfare takes on this sham fight with shadows, a cold war of weary words. There is no sense of shouting, rather of yawning. Laughter long ago stifled sobs in our assemblings together. Woe, woe, woe unto us for we have not submitted to sacrifice. We have not guessed the power of the calling to which God has called—its power to ruin and to revise, its strength to slay."[14]

Francis J. Roberts puts these words into the mouth of Jesus: "Do ye desire to follow me truly? Look for the blood-stained prints of my feet. Go, as it were, to the cold, unyielding rock in the Garden of Gethsemane, where self is put aside, and the cup of suffering is accepted. Die to thine own treacherous and deceiful heart. Rise with determination to go on unflinchingly, not hope to spare thyself. Save thy life and ye shall surely lose it. Offer it up to me, this very day, in a renewal of consecration unto sacrificial living, and I will accept thee and thou shalt know joy as new wine."[15]

So then, if I would be His disciple, I must decide what kind of follower I will be. Elliot saw an interesting parallel between the kind of persons Christ needs as His disciples and those hardy people who respond to the "call of the Yukon" (Service's *Law of the Yukon*):

> Send not your foolish and feeble; send me your strong and your sane.
>> Strong for the red-rage of battle; sane for I harry them sore.
>> Send me men girt for combat; men who are grit to the core.
>> Swift as the panther in triumph, fierce as the bear in defeat,
>> Sired of a bulldog parent, steeled in the furnace of heat . . .
> And I wait for the men who will win me—and I will not be won in a day,
>> And I will not be won by weaklings, subtle and suave and mild,

But by men with the hearts of Vikings and the simple faith of
a child,
   Desperate, strong, and resistless, unthrottled by fear or defeat.
   Them will I gild with my treasure, them will I glut with my meat."[16]

So then, I must be prepared for battle and for sacrifice, and I must
fan the spark that God put within me. I must be careful to distance
myself from everything that would tend to smother that spark.

The psalmist, David, wrote, "As the deer pants for the streams
of water, so pants my soul after thee, O God" (Ps. 42:1,2). A. W.
Tozer says, "to have found God and still to pursue Him is the soul's
paradox of love, scorned by the too-easily-satisfied religionist, but
justified in happy experience by the children of the burning heart."[17]
I must decide whether I will be a follower with a burning heart—
a true disciple of the Lord's.

## A Moment and a Lifetime

Finally, although I alone decide what kind of follower I will
be—whether the divine spark (theologians call it prevenient grace)
within me will be fanned into a flame or not—I must never forget,
as Tozer reminds us, "we pursue God because He has first put an
urge within us that spurs us to the pursuit."[18] I thank Him for His
call. I pray I shall never take it lightly.

It only takes a moment to answer Jesus' call, but it takes a lifetime to develop into a mature disciple. As the Apostle Paul says,
"until we all reach unity in the faith and in the knowledge of the
Son of God and become mature, attaining to the whole measure of
the fullness of Christ" (Eph. 4:13).

Now I have answered the call of Jesus to follow Him. I have
burned my boats and flung down the ladders, and I am determined
to cultivate the spiritual life within me. I will be watchful that
there are no competing loyalties and that I do not become entangled
in those things that will tend to put out the fire. Am I ready to live

a victorious life and be a witness for Christ in the world? Well, not quite. A disciple must be *filled with the Holy Spirit*. The Holy Spirit is God's gift to me and all His children. Have I been filled with the Holy Spirit? In the next chapter, we look carefully at this epochal spiritual experience.

## QUESTIONS FOR REFLECTION

1.  Why do some people seem to know God better and have a greater impact upon their world?

2.  Have I seriously thought about what kind of Christian or disciple that I want to be? Would I be satisfied with mediocrity in my spiritual life?

3.  What kind of appetite do I really have for God and things spiritual?

4.  What do I do, if anything, to cultivate those appetites, or do I simply ignore my spiritual hungers?

5.  Discuss the author's illustration of "picking blackberries" and its relationship to discipleship.

6.  Name some things that can "snag" us and keep us from becoming faithful and fruitful disciples?

7.  Discuss what Amy Carmichael means when she writes: "Can he have followed far who has no wound, nor scar?"

8.  What is the connection between the lines from Service's *Law of the Yukon* and discipleship?

# A PRAYER FOR SERIOUS FOLLOWERS

Lord, I thank you for the "spiritual receptivity" that you have tucked into my heart. I want to make it the biggest thing in my life. I want to be strong for the "red rage" of spiritual battle, and willing to be wounded and scarred for You—My Master.

Let me never fall prey to spiritual mediocrity. Deliver me from all that would entangle my feet and weight me down, for I must run this race and win it. I will follow the blood-stained prints of your feet, Dear Jesus. Amen.

# CHAPTER FOUR

# WILL I BE A SPIRIT-FILLED DISCIPLE?

*It's possible to be a believer and not have power; it's impossible to live the adventuresome life Christ intended without the Holy Spirit.*

—Lloyd John Ogilvie

*The gift of the Holy Spirit was to make the Spirit-filled people a gift to the world.*

—Lloyd John Ogilvie

Once the early disciples got past their own disbelief, the reality of the Risen Christ broke over them as surely as the tide was insistently kissing the Mediterranean seashore. They knew Jesus was alive and had ascended, and their joy could not be contained. They knew their faith had not been misplaced. They were indeed following the Messiah.

## A Great Commission—A Great Hesitation

They were now eager to fulfill the mandate of Jesus to "go and make disciples of all nations," but ironically, they were restrained by something else Jesus had said. They remembered that He had also told them *not to go*, but to *wait*. "Do not leave Jerusalem, but wait for the gift my Father promised which you have heard me speak about. For John baptized with water, but in a few days you will be baptized with the Holy Spirit . . . you will receive power when the Holy Spirit is come upon you and you shall be my witnesses" (Acts 1:4, 5, 8).

As Lloyd John Ogilvie reminds us, Jesus wanted his disciples to be "people who could wait for God, who would *allow God to work through them*, not people who would work for God on their own schedule and priorities."[1] "Waiting" is not something we are good at. We prefer to "do it ourselves." We suffer from what has been called the "little messiah" complex. But Jesus said, "wait."

"The difference between a spiritual man and a man who is not spiritual," says Oswald Chambers, "is just in this power to wait . . . the test of the strength of spiritual aspiration is—will I wait for God . . . do I believe Jesus Christ can turn me into His disciple if I let Him have His way."[2]

The disciples remembered also how Jesus had made clear to them on that wonderful, yet terrible night of His arrest, that He would not leave them as orphans in this world, but would give them another Comforter—the Holy Spirit. They did not fully understand it all, but obediently, and with expectancy, the disciples made their way to that now famous "Upper Room." Other followers of Jesus, now also convinced of His resurrection, began to join them until there were one hundred and twenty gathered in earnest prayer, thanking God, searching their hearts, and dedicating themselves anew to Him and the Kingdom which He had proclaimed.

Jesus did not disappoint them. Ten days later, true to His promise, God poured out His Spirit on those first disciples and shook that city and the world with what is known as Pentecost. Now, those disciples who had been plagued by quarreling, jealousy, bad attitudes, timidity, and cowardice before Pentecost, were suddenly transformed. They became bold, courageous witnesses for Jesus.

What was the difference? Acts 2:4 gives the answer. "All of them were filled with the Holy Spirit."

## Pentecost Is for Me Too

So what does it all mean to a twenty-first century, third-millennium Christian? It means that just as Jesus' first followers and disciples needed to be filled with the Holy Spirit, so also do *today's* disciples. They were already followers, *but they needed something else.* They needed what has been called *the fullness of the Spirit.*

There is a sense, of course, in which that first Pentecost is unrepeatable. It ushered in a new dispensation—the Age of the Spirit. But it is clear from the Bible and church history that God intends for each disciple in each generation, to have his or her own personal Pentecost.

Universalism wrongly teaches that since God gave His Son for the salvation of the world, everyone will be saved. A personal appropriation of God's grace through repentance and faith is deemed unnecessary. In like manner, some incorrectly view Pentecost. They reason: God poured out His Spirit at Pentecost; therefore all believers "have been filled with the Spirit."

Jesus speaks personally to His followers today as clearly as He did to those first-century disciples, saying, "wait for the gift my Father promised" (Acts 1:4b). Have I waited? Have I been filled with the Holy Spirit? As a committed follower of His, I want to be obedient. I know that I surely must need His promised gift as much as those first followers did. On the day of Pentecost, Peter said, "The promise is for you and your children and for all who are far off—for all whom the Lord our God will call" (Acts 2:39).

Just as some of the information available to us on our computers is limited in usefulness until we *download* it, so likewise many of the resources and promises of God wait to be "downloaded" by His children. In regard to Pentecost, God asks, "Have you clicked onto the download button and received the full implications and blessings of Pentecost for your personal life?"

When we are first converted, free from guilt, and walking in the fresh glow of "new life in Christ," like those post-resurrection disciples so intoxicated with the Risen Christ, we may not immediately realize our need, but sooner or later (often painfully soon) we discover that there is an unholy warfare going on in our hearts—the mind of Christ and the carnal mind are in a life-and-death struggle. God yet has a cleansing for that carnal mind. It happens when we are *filled* with His Spirit.

A. J. Gordon writes, "it seems clear from the Scriptures that it is still the duty and privilege of *believers* to receive the Holy Spirit by a conscious, definite act of appropriating faith, just as they received Christ . . . for it is as sinners that we accept Christ for our justification, but it is as *sons* that we accept the Spirit for our sanctification."[3]

## Pentecost Is A Special Gift for God's Children

Being filled with the Holy Spirit is a crisis experience of grace that generally follows conversion. It was for the original disciples themselves. It was for the Samaritan believers (Acts 8). It was for the Apostle Paul (Acts 9:17). It was for the Gentile believers at Caesarea (Acts 10:44, 45), and it was for the Ephesians (Acts 19:6).

When Paul says to the Ephesians, "Do not be drunk with wine . . . but be filled with the Spirit" (Eph. 5:18), he is writing to those who are already believers, *but not yet filled with the Spirit.* Indeed as W. T. Purkiser reminds us, "The letters of the New Testament are all addressed to *Christians.* They were written *within the context of faith* and directed to those who had been converted . . . whatever is urged upon them must, therefore, be understood as part of what follows the initial experience of salvation."[4] In the New Testament, sinners are always exhorted to repent, while believers are urged to be *filled with the Spirit.*

Christ Himself clarifies who is a candidate for being filled with the Holy Spirit, when in His great discourse on the Holy Spirit, He says, "If you love me, you will obey what I command. And I will ask the Father, and He will give you another Counselor to be with you forever—The Spirit of Truth. The *world* cannot accept him, because it neither sees him nor knows him. But you know him for he lives with you and will be in you" (Jn. 14:15–17, emphasis mine).

## Harmony in the History of Great Saints

James Gilchrist Lawson, author of the classic work, *Deeper Experiences of Famous Christians,* spent years in the greatest libraries of Europe and America, seeking to understand and describe the most spiritual and helpful Christian experiences of those who were preeminent for their piety and spiritual power. Lawson says that "there is a wonderful harmony in the experiences related. The persons described . . . relate their deeper experiences in very different terms; but the deeper Christian experience described is always the same. It is the baptism, or filling, or gift of the Holy Spirit and the experience resulting from being "filled with the Spirit."[5]

Lawson explains that the "Methodist may describe this deeper experience as 'entire sanctification,' 'holiness,' or 'perfect love.' The Baptist may call it the 'baptism of the Holy Spirit' or the 'filling of the Spirit.' The Presbyterian may call it the 'life of faith' or the 'rest of faith,' or the 'full assurance of the faith' . . . the Quaker may call it 'living in the Spirit,' or 'walking in the Spirit,' or 'overcoming power' . . . all refer to a Spirit-filled Christian experience."[6]

Lawson believes that there is "practical agreement among those who believe in a deeper Christian experience than conversion." He says "all agree that Christians may be 'filled with the Spirit.'"[7] They not only *may*, but *must* be filled if they are to be cleansed, empowered, guided into all truth, comforted and made a comfort to others, enabled to endure persecution and suffering, and are to become effective witnesses for Christ.

## I Must Choose to Be Filled with the Holy Spirit

So as a follower of Christ, I have to consciously decide whether or not I will be a Spirit-filled disciple. Are there Christian believers who have not been filled with the Spirit. Richard Taylor answers: "Not only is it possible to be saved without being filled with the Spirit, but also it is possible to cease being filled with the Spirit without ceasing to be saved. Many a once-Spirit-filled Christian, once alive with spiritual power, is now walking in the doldrums, yet plugging away in average Christianity."[8]

In that beautiful discussion with His disciples about prayer, Jesus said, "Ask and it will be given to you; seek and you will find; knock and the door will be opened to you. For everyone who asks receives; he who seeks finds; and to him who knocks, the door will be opened. . . . If you then . . . know how to give good gifts to your children, how much more will your Father in heaven give the Holy Spirit to those who ask him!" (Lk. 11:9, 10, 13b, emphasis mine).

Richard Taylor emphasizes, "This is a discussion of the relationship of children to parents. The promise of the Holy Spirit is to God's children, who need the gift of the Holy Spirit in His sanctifying presence and power."[9] Apparently Jesus knows that the Holy Spirit is as much a basic necessity for His children as bread is for our children in the flesh.

Being aware of His promise and my own need, and making a full consecration of my life to Him, prepares me to ask for His Spirit. *Asking* is a prerequisite, for as Richard Taylor points out, "The Father will not overwhelm us by an outpouring of the Spirit for which we have not asked. This is a gift that is never forced on anyone."[10]

"Asking" is necessary, but asking may be done with the wrong motive. When, however, I begin to seriously ask for God to fill me with His Spirit, He will show me whether or not I am prepared to receive this Holy Person into my heart and life. He will not come into a heart that is unsurrendered or one that is cluttered with unforgiveness or resentment.

Peter clearly defines the condition for being filled with the Spirit. The Holy Spirit is given to "those who obey" (Acts 5:32). Lloyd John Ogilvie writes, "Obedience is like a thermostat. It opens the flow of the Spirit for the needs around us. The cold of the world calls for the heat and warmth of the fire of the Holy Spirit within us."[11]

Was that first Pentecost given according to a fixed date on God's calendar, or was it the climax of private heart searching and relational reconciliation among those first followers? I believe it was the latter. God does not give His Holy Spirit to hearts filled with resentments, reservations, unforgiveness and defensiveness.

Taylor says, "Let us push past our fears until we are able to say from the heart:

"Father, give me the gift of Your Spirit as my Comforter, Guide, Teacher, Sanctifier. I want Him to search every nook and cranny and cleanse everything He finds wrong. I turn over all the keys. Not one is held back. I will seek His guidance in all things. I will let Him eliminate from my life any person, or any plan, or any association He does not approve. I will be clay in His hands. I will go where He wants me to go and stay where He wants me to stay. I will back up when He tells me to back up. I will make apologies when He rebukes me. I will be willing not to be in the limelight. I will let Him give me whatever success He wants me to have. I will seek to do His work in His way—the way of prayer, holiness, faith, and obedience. I will not grab the reins out of His hands and drive down my own paths. And above all, Lord, *cleanse my heart from the nature that wants to whittle this down* just a little—which is putting up a fight just now. I let go of myself; please take over."[12]

You get the idea. It may be a prayer in my own words, but it must be a prayer that comes from deep surrender and that sincerely offers my all on God's altar. Praying such a prayer will prepare the heart to claim God's promise of the gift *in faith*.

Whether I am a new Christian believer, or have been a follower of Jesus for sometime, if I have not been filled with the Holy Spirit, I can be. I can have a testimony like Faye—the woman described in the next section.

## I Got the Rest of It

The Sunday evening message was over. I had preached on man's need of a pure heart. The congregation was singing "I Surrender All." They had not sung long when an attractive, nicely dressed lady in her senior years stepped out into the sanctuary aisle. I recognized her as a lady who had only recently started attending our church with a friend.

She made her way slowly, but deliberately to the front of the church. Her eyes were fixed on me, and she didn't stop at the altar, but came near to the pulpit as if she wanted to speak to me personally.

She said softly, "I don't understand all about it, but I want all that God has for me." I directed her to kneel at the altar nearby and called for several ladies to come forward to pray with Faye.

The altar call continued. Others came, and soon the invitation was closed. The scene that followed indicates how simple faith can get the Lord's attention. I heard Faye say simply, "Lord, give me more; I want more." God always hears such earnest petitions for more of Himself, and that's exactly what He did for Faye.

Following the altar service, people were standing to testify of God's faithfulness. Faye stood to her feet and spoke clearly. What she said was, *"I got the rest of it."* She went on, "I've been a Christian for many years, and I've tried to do what is right, but I haven't been taught about being filled with the Spirit, or sanctification in my church, or if I was, it didn't take on me, but I think this may be why God directed me to this church. I am so happy."

Since Faye had been a member of another church for years, I did not encourage her to change her membership, but she read additional material and prayed and several weeks later did unite with our church saying, "God told me 'this is where I want you.'"

She read books on Christian holiness and began witnessing to and bringing her family and friends to the services.

One has to wonder how many people like Faye are out there, just waiting for a neighbor friend, co-worker, or loved one to invite them to a Spirit-filled service, so that they too can "get the rest of it." Actually, it is not so much my getting the rest of it, as it is *God getting the rest of me.*

A. B. Simpson wrote: "Oh, for a race of Pauls! Oh for an army of Gideons! Oh, for a band of heroes! Oh, for the baptism of the Holy Spirit in all the meaning of Pentecost and in all the highest thought of Christ Himself."[13]

What difference will the Holy Spirit make in my life. Will I have power to live victoriously for Christ? In the next chapter we will explore the nature of the change being filled with the Holy Spirit makes in one's life.

## QUESTIONS FOR REFLECTION

1.  Have I seriously considered why Jesus promised to give the Holy Spirit to His disciples?

2.  What specific instructions did Jesus give His first disciples regarding being filled with the Holy Spirit?

3.   Have I considered Jesus' promise important enough to have my own personal "tryst of waiting"?

4.   Have I personally asked Jesus for the gift of the Holy Spirit? (Lk. 11:10)

5.   Have I *received* the promised Gift?

6.   Have I ever witnessed to this filling?

7.   If you have asked, and not received the Holy Spirit, consider again what makes one a candidate for receiving this special Gift?

---

## A PRAYER FOR SERIOUS FOLLOWERS

Jesus, you spoke of the gift of the Holy Spirit as "the promise of the Father." You commanded your first disciples to wait for that promise, and you did not disappoint them, but filled them with the Holy Spirit at Pentecost.

I know that you will not disappoint me, or any of your followers today who will wait for and ask for their own personal pentecost. Peter said the promise was not only for the "first" disciples, but for "all who are afar off—for all whom the Lord our God will call."

Thank you, Jesus, for not only calling us to discipleship, but equipping us with your very Spirit so that we could be your witnesses. I welcome the fullness of the Spirit into my heart and life right now. Amen.

# CHAPTER FIVE

# WHAT KIND OF POWER AM I PROMISED?

*It is a terrible thing to have a passion with no power to live it.*
—Lloyd John Ogilvie

*It is not your power, but His power. It is not abstract power under your control, but it is a Person . . . He has the power and you have Him.*
—A. B. Simpson

Whether one is buying a vehicle, a tool, or a new computer, he wants to know: Will it have the power to do the job? Likewise, every new convert or new disciple wants to know, "Will I have the power I need to stand up for Christ, to resist temptation, to witness for Him, to endure persecution for His cause, and to accomplish the work He calls me to do?

As a Spirit-filled follower of Jesus, I know what Jesus said to His disciples following His resurrection—"You will receive *power* when the Holy Spirit comes on you, and you will be my witnesses . . ." (Acts 1:8, emphasis mine). So I know that Jesus promised power, and that the power He promised is associated with the Holy Spirit, so it must be *spiritual* power.

Now, raw power is something the generations of the twentieth century have witnessed. What generations in this planet's history could boast of having both shuddered at the detonations of the atomic and hydrogen bombs, and thrilled at the seven million pounds of thrust that lifted Neil Armstrong and his fellow astronauts onto the lunar surface?

The new century is likely to bring even more breathtaking kinds of power—the towing of icebergs to provide fresh water for dry climates, the development of "beam weapons" to generate gravitational collapse, 100 trillion calculations a second, and computers the size of a grain of sand, to mention only a few.

The apostle Paul, not having witnessed any of these developments, but inspired by the Holy Spirit, spoke of an *incomparably great power*—greater than all of the above. Paul explained, it is "like the working of his mighty strength, which he exerted in Christ when he raised him from the dead and seated him at his right hand in the heavenly realms, far above all . . . power . . . not only in this present age but also in the one to come (Eph. 1:19).

A. Skevington Wood, declared "In an age which worships power, we do well to remind ourselves that all the incredible energies locked up in the atom are as nothing and less than nothing compared with the supernatural might which brought back Jesus from the dead."[1]

## God's Power—The Unique Power We Need

As impressive as the harnessing of natural power and the achievements of modern technology are, man is always more profoundly impressed by a power that can absolve his guilt, conquer his passions, equip him to face everyday life, and prepare him for eternity.

The apostle Paul cried out for a power that could overrule the power of sin within him. He said, "What a wretched man I am!

Who will rescue me from this body of death?" His answer to his own question was, "Thanks be to God—through Jesus Christ our Lord" (Rom. 7:24,25). Paul had personally experienced the "resurrection power" of Jesus that alters disposition and behavior, and he knew that there was *no greater power.*

This resurrection power of Jesus was both a power to *be* or *to become,* and a power to *achieve* or to *accomplish.* Both require a divine cleansing, and a divine indwelling. First we look at the power *to be.*

## God's Power Is the Power "To Be"—Like Christ

The power I most need if I am to follow Christ and be His disciple is the power *to be. Being* always trumps *doing* of course. Even quite apart from the spiritual perspective, we easily prefer a person whom we believe to be a "good" man or woman—let's say one who is trustworthy, dependable, and kind, over one who may be an accomplished musician, a great performer, or say, a talented athlete, but who does not manifest the "character" virtues or simple graciousness.

"Even Gibbon, the infidel historian, confessed that the chief secret of the early triumph of Christianity was the pure and victorious lives of early Christians. There is no argument against a good life," wrote A. B. Simpson, "Our first need, therefore, is power to overcome sin and manifest the virtues and attractions of goodness, love, patience, and self-sacrifice."[2]

Richard Taylor writes: "Every Christian can and should be an example of divine grace, a wonder to angels and demons, an amazement to watching men. And the more feeble a Christian is in *himself,* the more pronounced his power should be, for God said to Paul, 'my strength is made perfect in weakness.'"[3]

The power we most need is the power *be like Christ.* It doesn't matter what miracles I can perform or what great and successful work I might do for the Lord if in fact I do not bear the *imago Christi*—the image of Christ. C. S. Lewis wrote: "Men are mirrors, or 'carriers' of Christ to other men. . . . The church exists for no other purpose, but to draw men into Christ, to make them little Christs . . . God became man for no other purpose. It is even doubtful, you know, whether the whole universe was created for any other reason."[4]

Now *if I am to be like Christ, I must, of course, know what Christ was like*—so I know what virtues and qualities should characterize my life. Certainly the world's libraries are filled with glowing descriptions of our Lord and Master, mostly based upon the Bible— our primary source. Indeed a good starting point in Bible reading for new converts or disciples is the gospels—Matthew, Mark, Luke and John—the inspired historical documents recording the life and ministry of Jesus Christ.

Certainly, the beautiful character of Christ cannot be captured in a "short list" of His sterling qualities, but we would surely have to begin with His absolute *purity* and *holiness*. We could not fail to observe His *love* for both His disciples and also for sinners, but foremost—His love for His Father and His Father's will.

No one could miss the *servant-spirit* of Jesus who said, "the Son of Man did not come to be served, but to serve, and to give his life as a ransom for many" (Mt. 20:28). Nor could one ignore the *spirit of prayer* that permeated all His work of ministry. Many other flawless virtues such as *mercy, compassion, kindness, gentleness,* and *fairness,* characterized His life. And always these virtues were held in a balanced way. Indeed, His life was a model—a divine template of His own teaching in the Sermon on the Mount.

## To Be Like Christ Requires More Than a Self-help Regimen

The more difficult challenge is *how* to get Christ-like qualities to characterize *my* life. It is not difficult at all to identify those qualities in Jesus, but I cannot just *decide* to imitate His virtues and expect it to happen. The infection stemming from Adam's sin has corrupted every human heart with what theologians call *original sin.*

For that sin I need a power beyond myself—and that is precisely why I need the cleansing work of the Holy Spirit. Theologian H. Ray Dunning, says, "The purpose of the infilling of the Spirit is to transform life into Christlikeness . . . the Spirit serves many functions as the Agent of God's work in the world, but in His sanctifying function He indwells the believer to produce within Him and in his life the character of Jesus Christ"

Dunning continues, "He produces in us the radical virtues of Christ, such as radical humility, radical forgiveness, radical love, radical power (the power of suffering love, not force), and radical Christlikeness."[5]

J. Kenneth Grider says the Baptism with the Holy Spirit is the "fulfillment of the prayer of Jesus for His disciples: 'Sanctify them' (Jn. 17:17)," and he states further, "The Holy Spirit indwells the believer pervasively. In that same instant, original sin is cleansed away. Indeed, it is this very baptism with fire that cleanses . . . the perverse, recalcitrant, estranging state of original sin—for the indwelling sin (Rom 7:17,20) must be expelled in order for the Holy Spirit to indwell the believer in such fullness."[6]

Grider also quotes Adam Clarke, that distinguished theologian and contemporary of John Wesley, who wrote: "God promised his Holy Spirit to sanctify and cleanse the heart, so as utterly to destroy all pride, anger, self-will . . . and everything contrary to his own holiness. . . . He is also the sanctifying spirit . . . and as such he condemns to utter destruction the whole of the carnal mind."[7]

While this certainly cannot be a complete study on Christian holiness, it is important for every disciple to know that God has provided a divine means for cleansing the heart so that His followers can bear His image to the world. John Wesley said, "you know the great end of religion is to renew our hearts in the image of God, to repair that total loss of righteousness and true holiness which we sustained by the sin of our first parents."[8]

Again Dunning writes, "Wesley learned that sanctification is a lifelong process that includes an instantaneous moment at which one is perfected in love. . . . After carefully examining the testimonies of numerous persons, he reached the conclusion that all had experienced the great transformation in an instant. True, this moment was both preceded and followed by gradual sanctification or growth in grace, *but the actual deliverance from inward sin was instantaneous.*"[9]

This is the first part of the power which the Holy Spirit brings. As George Shaw writes, "Purity is power, and there is no greater preparation for the service of the Master than a thoroughly cleansed soul."[10] But there is a second part to this power—it is the power *to do*.

## The Power *To Do* or *To Achieve*—For Christ

Jesus made it clear that when we are filled with the Holy Spirit, *we will be His witnesses* (Acts 1:8). Jesus also gave to His disciples a mandate, called the Great Commission: "All authority in heaven and on earth has been given to me. Therefore go and make disciples of all nations, baptizing them in the name of the Father and of the Son and of the Holy Spirit, and teaching them to obey everything I have commanded you. And surely I am with you always, to the very end of the age" (Mt. 28:18–20).

Those first-century Christian believers took Jesus seriously and their "acts" (deeds) certainly gave clear evidence of having been endued with a heavenly power that energized their testimony and every area of their lives.

A. M. Hills wrote: "The early disciples had no wealth, no social position, no prestige, no government aid, no help from established institutions. They were in themselves a despised and feeble folk, without influence, without skill, without education, without a New Testament, or even the Old Testament in the hands of the people, without a Christian literature, or a single Christian house of worship. Pomp, power, custom and public sentiment were all against them. They were reproached, reviled, persecuted, and subjected to exile and death.

"But those early Christians had the help of an indwelling, sanctifying Savior and the anointing of the Holy Ghost, and with that equipment they faced a hostile world and all the malignant powers of darkness and conquered. Within seventy years, according to the smallest estimate, there were half a million followers of Jesus . . . in other words, with Holy Spirit power upon them they increased more than four thousand fold in threescore years."[11]

One surely has to acknowledge that *here* was power *to achieve.* It was a power to overcome enormous obstacles and opposition, and to not only persevere in their faith personally and individually, but here was the power of grace spreading out like a flooding river, fulfilling the mandate of the Master.

Clearly that power was rooted in their likeness to their Master—*imago Christi,* but it translated into a power to accomplish specific tasks and goals. Their power of witness was not just passive, but *active.* How else could one interpret the book of *Acts?*

"And with great power gave the apostles witness of the resurrection of the Lord Jesus: and great grace was upon them all" (Acts 4:33, KJV).

## It Is the Power to Speak for Christ

There are thousands of Christians who are fearful of speaking for Jesus, or leading a prayer time, or who cannot lead a soul to Christ. Dwight Moody once wrote something that seems to be as true today as it was when he wrote it. He said, "nine-tenths, at least, of the church members never think of speaking for Christ. If they see a man, perhaps a near relative, just going right down to ruin, going rapidly, they never think of speaking to him about his sinful course, and of seeking to win him to Christ. Now certainly there must be something wrong. And yet, when you talk with them, you find they have faith, and you cannot say they are not children of God, but they have not the power, they have not the liberty, they have not the love that real disciples should have."[12]

Considering the remedy for this situation, Moody continued, "A great many people are thinking that we need new measures, that we need new churches, that we need new organs, new choirs, all these things. That is not what the church of God needs today. It is the old power that the Apostles had; that is what we want, and if we have that in our churches, there will be new life, then we will have new ministers—the same old ministers renewed with power, filled with the Spirit. . . . Oh that God may anoint His people! Not the ministry only but every disciple."[13]

Certainly not everyone filled with the Holy Spirit will have the gift of evangelism, but God will impart courage to His disciples to open their lips and speak up for Him. The Holy Spirit empowers the *lips* as well as the *lives* of Jesus' disciples. The fullness of the Spirit will always impart a passion for prayer and for souls, and a greater love for the work of God through His church.

## It Is the Power to Create Fellowship and Unity

We read in Acts that the disciples "devoted themselves to the apostles' teaching and to the fellowship, to the breaking of bread and to prayer . . . all the believers were together and had everything in common. . . . Every day they continued to meet together . . . they broke bread in their homes and ate together with glad and sincere hearts, praising God and enjoying the favor of all the people. And the Lord added to their number daily those who were being saved" (Acts 2:42–47).

The power to make people *one* is not the result of human striving. Pentecost performed the miracle of unity among the apostles and all the disciples. The fire of the Holy Spirit not only cleanses the individual's heart, but becomes a *galvanizing* medium within the body of believers. Lloyd John Ogilvie writes: "Welding takes white-hot fire. The fire in my heart coupled with the fire in yours makes us one. The union is intellectual as we receive the mind of Christ; it is emotional as we feel the warmth of love for each other in spite of hurts or failures; and it's volitional as we make decisions to do His will together. *Christ prayed* that we might be one."[14]

Spirit-filled power is what Richard Taylor calls "*overflowing love* that reaches up for more of God and reaches out for lost souls. Such love," says Taylor, "rises above the shabby and petty to be redemptive."[15] Such love creates the spiritual unity that characterized the post-Pentecost disciples. Spirit-filled unity always amazes the world. The lack of it insults and embarrasses the Lord of the church.

## Power to Write a New *"Acts of the Disciples"*

The Holy Spirit is the "glorified Christ" indwelling and impelling His followers in everyday life and in unimaginable achievements of victory. The acts of the Apostles may be completed, but the "acts of Christ's disciples" are not. The story goes on. You and I are to be the instruments through which the Holy Spirit continues His exciting work in the third millennium. How many years of the new century or the new millennium we have before Christ returns in a final consummation of time, no one knows, but we can be sure that He wants us to be fully equipped in order to glorify Him and to fulfill the mission He gave to us.

Ogilvie writes: "God's new age of Pentecost in our time will happen when we understand the Holy Spirit, long for the Holy Spirit, pray for the Holy Spirit, and open ourselves to the Holy Spirit as the contemporary Christ with us and within us."[16]

Great spiritual power is available to the disciples of Jesus today, but I must never lose sight of the true nature of that power. It is *the power of brokenness.*

## God's Power Is the Power of Brokenness

Holy Spirit power is different from secular and worldly power. We must never forget that. In his book, *Loving God,* Charles Colson recounts a moving story from the life of Aleksandr Solzhenitsyn. As a prisoner of the Soviet state, Solzhenitsyn's life was one of back-breaking labor and slow starvation in the fields.

One day, when hopelessness had engulfed him, Solzhenitsyn slumped down on a crude worksite bench. He knew that any moment he would be ordered up, and if he didn't respond he could be bludgeoned to death with his own shovel.

While waiting with his head bowed, Solzhenitsyn felt a "presence." Slowly he lifted his eyes to discover next to him an old man. Hunched over, the old man drew a stick through the sand at Solzhenitsyn's feet, *tracing the outline of a cross.*

As Solzhenitsyn stared at that cross in the sand, his entire perspective changed. It gave him hope. Although he realized that he was only one man against the powerful Soviet empire—yet in that moment he saw clearly that the hope of mankind was in the Cross, and through that power *anything* was possible.

Solzhenitsyn slowly picked up his shovel and went back to work, not knowing that one day his writings on truth and freedom would enflame the world. Such is the power of the cross—the power of brokenness.[17]

## The True Meaning of the Cross Is Brokenness

The cross is worshipped and enshrined. It is worn on lapels and gold chains, and is lifted high on the steeple, yet adorns the necks of people afraid to die. The world doesn't understand *bro-*

*kenness* as power. It is not very appealing either to the common man or the ruling classes of any society. Society is obsessed with its own brand of power.

Even Jesus was not without temptation here. Frequently He was asked to exhibit His power, but Jesus did not fall for the ruse, and was never distracted from the centrality of the Cross, and the brokenness that was necessary to save lost mankind.

Simple words from Jesus may explain the power of the Cross and the gospel.

Inviting His disciples to partake of and better understand the sacrament of His whole life, death, and resurrection, Jesus said, "This is my body, *which is broken for you*" (1 Cor. 11:24, KJV italics mine). The power of Jesus lay in His *brokenness.*

Charles Colson said of his own life, "All my life I sought wealth, success, and fame because they were the keys, or so I thought, to security and power." Colson, however found what so many have found—these are only the *illusions* of power. "I was blind," he said. "Indeed only in the breakdown of power did I finally understand both it and myself."[18]

In the midst of the epochal changes in today's culture and affluence, Christian believers and church leaders alike have too often lost sight of the true power of the gospel. Maybe we are acting too much like the political and financial power brokers of today?

While we don't easily admit it, the Church (and we are the church) has adopted many of the attitudes and methods of the secular models of power. But the Holy Spirit power will never be ours or return to the church until we change our reference point. How can we exchange the illusion of power for the real power? How can we become "brokers" of brokenness?

*We must partake of His brokenness.* We can do this by first looking at Jesus and His sacrifice. By looking at the cross. Not the steepled cross, or the delicate, necklaced cross—but *the ugly cross* of Calvary where Jesus was subjected to the most brutal brokenness possible. We will never be broken by watching the world and copying its concepts of power. We'll never be broken by watching one another. Pride is too subtle and human templates crack. We must watch *Jesus*.

***How do we watch Jesus?*** Through serious study of His Word, through prayer, through worship, and by a reverent participation in the Sacrament of the Lord's Supper. This is "chosen" brokenness. The great revivals of the world have been born in times of fervent prayer and repentance. Repentance is the brokenness that God always responds to and blesses.

When Jesus said, "You shall receive power when the Holy Spirit has come upon you," He was not promising "worldly" or "secular" power, but *spiritual* power—the power of love and brokenness. He was promising the power to be broken like He was broken.

Do I know Christ not only in the power of His resurrection, but also in "the fellowship of sharing in his sufferings, becoming like him in his death"? (Phil. 3:10). *Suffering.* Ugh, there is that word few in this world would choose, but the Christian must. Contrary to a comfortable gospel of health, wealth, and prosperity, Christ offered His followers a *cross*. The cross always involves suffering, but it leads to resurrection and the crown.

Jim Elliot, who along with four other young missionaries was speared to death in efforts to get the gospel to the Auca Indians in Equador, once penned in his journal: "We are sheep of His pasture. Enter into His gates with thanksgiving, and into His courts with praise. And what are sheep doing going into the gate? What is their purpose inside these courts? To bleat melodies and enjoy the company of the flock? *No, these sheep were destined for the altar.* Their pasture feeding had been for one purpose, to test them and fatten them for bloody sacrifice. Give Him thanks, then, that you have been counted worthy of His altars."[19]

## I Need Not Be Without Spiritual Power

As a disciple of Jesus it is great to know that I have been promised the power that I will need to keep illuminated by the Light of the World and energized by heaven's eternal dynamo—God's Son.

On Thursday, August 14, 2003, 50 million people in northeastern United States and in southern Canada found out what it is like to be without "light" and "power." A huge, sudden "blackout" exposed people to stifling heat, clogged rush-hour streets with millions of people and cars trying to move without traffic signals. People were trapped in skyscraper elevators, New York City subways, and in mines deep in the earth. Some major airports were virtually shut down. Broadway and thousands of business were idled by rolling power outages.

While "electrical" power is generated in many places, it is transmitted through interconnected power grids or control centers that can monitor electrical demands over large areas and can reroute power from areas of low demand to those of higher demand.

That may ordinarily be good for American power consumers, but in some cases, there can be a cascading of outages such as experienced on August 14th. The good news for Jesus' disciples is that we have a *direct* line to our source of power—Jesus. My principal source of spiritual power is not dependent upon someone else's, and I need not fear an interruption of power from some remote power grid failure. I need only keep Jesus on the throne of my heart and life, and keep filled with His Spirit. *He is my light and my power!*

Equipped then with the power of the Holy Spirit, I must now turn my attention to some *disciplines* that will be necessary if I am to persevere in this spiritual journey with Jesus. I would want not only grace to endure, but grace to grow in likeness to my Master. Read on for some secrets gleaned from God's Word and from "saint watching."

# QUESTIONS FOR REFLECTION

1. Do I understand the nature of *spiritual* power? Discuss the different kinds of power in the world.

2. What kind of power is humankind most in awe of?

3. Which is most important—the power to *be*, or the power to *do* or *achieve*?

4. What is meant by the "power of brokenness"?

5. Why is the power of brokenness not attractive to most persons?

6. In what ways do we witness the abuse of power in the world?

7. Is spiritual power ever abused? How?

8. In what ways have I observed spiritual power at work in my own life?

# A PRAYER FOR SERIOUS FOLLOWERS

Father, in a power-hungry world, I would desire only the power to be like Jesus, and to accomplish your will for my life. Deliver me from all illusions and abuses of power. Let me understand and experience true spiritual power—the power of brokenness.

Thank you, Father, for counting me worthy to be one of your lambs, sacrificed for the redemption of the world. In Jesus' name, Amen.

# CHAPTER SIX

# ARE THERE ANY SECRETS FOR FINISHING THIS RACE?

*The conversion of a soul is the miracle of a moment, the manufacture of a saint is the task of a lifetime.*

—Alan Redpath

*There is not that thing in the world of more grave and urgent importance, throughout the life of man, than is discipline.*

—John Milton

*It is the great stern call of Jesus that fascinates men and women quicker than anything.*

—Oswald Chambers

Having begun a race is no assurance that one can win or even finish that race. As a young boy growing up, I soon discovered that when I raced with my neighborhood pals and schoolyard chums, I would often do very well getting to the finish line first.

I was, however, only briefly involved in any organized field and track events, and that in the eighth grade, and then we moved to a large city high school. One evening in my late high school years I happened by a practice session of the school track team. Just for fun, I ran a race or two with the sprinters. My time amazed them and they asked me if I wanted to accompany them to a track meet in another city that week-end. I agreed.

Now the story gets better—or *worse*. Apparently one of their regular runners for the mile relay team was unable to race, and at the last moment they stuck me in that slot. The problem was, I not only was *not* a "relay trackster," but I had not even been practicing or disciplining myself for the 100-yard dash, much less for a 440 yard run.  Well, when I got that baton in my hand, I was "out of there," running the 440 like I ran the 100-yard dash. I'm sure at first, the spectators were wondering where they got this "coming Olympic star." After the first 150 yards, however I began to fade fast. By the time I reached the last 100 yards, not only was there little energy left, but my legs became uncontrollable. I had pushed myself too hard too long. When I finally stumbled over to the side of the track, I was very weak and very sick.

It's embarrassing now to think that I was that dumb, but the story illustrates beautifully that if one is going to run a race—any race, discipline and training are necessary. If it is a "marathon," such as the Christian race, *pacing* also becomes an important strategy.

God had blessed me with the gift of "fleetness," but I had not been a good steward of my gift. I had not been prepared. I had not been instructed. Which is one reason I am writing this book on discipleship. Too often we assume that people are automatically aware of the basics of discipleship, but they are not.

## The Disciple Must Run the Race and Finish it

In seeking to follow Jesus, there are many who shoot out of the "starting blocks" like high-spirited race horses, only to quickly fade or drop out of the race altogether. Jesus' parable of the soils should inform us here. "Some people are like seed along the path, where the word is sown. As soon as they hear it, Satan comes and takes away the word that was sown in them. Others, like seed sown on rocky places, hear the word and at once receive it with joy. But since they have no root, they last only a short time. When trouble or persecution comes because of the word, they quickly fall away. Still others, like seed sown among thorns, hear the word; but the worries of this life, the deceitfulness of wealth and the desires for other things come in and choke the word, making it unfruitful. Others, like seed sown on good soil, hear the word, accept it, and produce a crop—thirty, sixty or even a hundred times what was sown" (Mk. 4:15–20).

A disciple must be a learner, and there are many things to learn if I would follow Jesus through to the finish line. God has gifted me with "the call to follow Him." God has blessed me with forgiveness and "regenerating grace." "If anyone is in Christ: he is a new creation; the old has gone, the new has come!" (2 Cor. 5:17).

God has gifted me with His Spirit and enabled me to decide that I don't want to be a mediocre Christian—that I want my Christian life to make a difference in this world for Him

Thank God for His gifts, but I am responsible for what I do with God's gifts. Living the Christian life is not "all-of-God, and none-of-me," nor is it "all-of-me, and none-of-God," but a beautiful synthesis of "God *and* me."

There are some "disciplines" that I must cultivate—some training I must acquire if I am to persevere as a follower of Jesus. If I am to finish this spiritual journey—this marvelous marathon—I must learn to see *discipline* in the word, *disciple*.

Calvin Miller says, "Grace is God's gift to us, but discipline is our gift to him . . . and not to Him alone. Discipline is also a rare and vibrant pledge to ourselves. In the consecration of ourselves as living sacrifices, our own study and industry will provide us with a lifetime of rewards, and the gold will be ours."[1]

# WHAT DISCIPLINES WILL I NEED TO PERSEVERE?

**THERE IS THE DISCIPLINE OF WHAT GOD HAS WRITTEN— THE BIBLE.** How reassuring to know that we have a *speaking* God. God "spoke" and the world came into existence (Gen. 1). God spoke to Adam and Eve in the Garden before "the Fall" (Gen. 2:15), and after "the Fall" (Gen. 3:9). God spoke to Abraham, giving him a great promise (Gen. 12:1–3) and God spoke to Moses, giving him a difficult but thrilling assignment. (Ex. 3). God spoke to Samuel and to David and to all of the prophets, and they communicated with the people saying, "Thus saith the Lord."

But God not only "spoke" His word and will to the people, He had much of what He spoke recorded in *written* form and carefully preserved through the ages so that mankind would have more than an "oral tradition." It would be difficult enough in a fallen world to preserve the "written" Word, but even more difficult to preserve an oral tradition.

The Old and New Testaments have come to us through at least 40 different authors spanning some 1500 years. In one of the Apostle Peter's letters to the Early Church, he says, "Above all, you must understand that no prophecy of Scripture came about by the prophet's own interpretation. For prophecy never had its origin in the will of man, but men spoke from God as they were carried along by the Holy Spirit" (2 Pet. 1:20–21).

If I am to be a serious follower of Jesus, I must study the inspired accounts of His life and ministry as recorded in the gospels of *Matthew, Mark, Luke, and John.* I must also saturate myself in the history of the New Testament church as recorded in the *Acts of the Apostles* and the epistles or letters that Paul, Peter, and John wrote in the context of the early church.

Everyone's hero, Helen Keller, blind and deaf from infancy, said, "but how shall I speak of the glories I have since discovered in the Bible? For years I have read it with an ever-broadening sense of joy and inspiration; and I love it as I love no other book."[2]

**The Bible Must Be Our Canon of Conduct in All of Life.** Charles Ryrie says, "only in the Bible do we have truth that is indisputably reliable. For this reason, the Bible must be the guide and test for all our experiences in the spiritual life, for biblical spirituality is the only genuine spirituality."[3]

There is a *unity* to the Bible. Human history as a whole is the saga of the struggle of "fallen mankind" to recover joy in the midst of sorrow, hope in the midst of despair, and life in the midst of death.

The Bible provides that joy, hope, and life. It has been called "The Unfolding Drama of Redemption." W. Graham Scroggie writes: "Of this Drama of Redemption, the Earth is the Stage, Man and Nations are the *Dramatis Personae*, and Christ, let it be said most reverently, is the Hero."[4]

The history of Jesus Christ as disclosed in the New Testament, was revealed in the Old Testament *prophetically*. Christ dominates the entire revelation—old and new. Christ is the sum and substance of the Bible.

**Reading and Studying the Bible Is an Encounter with God.** Blackaby writes, "The Bible describes God's complete revelation of Himself to humanity. It is the record of God's dealings with humanity and His words to them. God speaks to you through the Bible . . . a person cannot understand spiritual truth unless the Spirit of God reveals it. In fact, the Holy Spirit is the Spirit of truth . . . understanding spiritual truth does not lead you to an encounter with God; *it is the encounter with God.*[5]

So, reading and studying the Bible is an encounter with God as surely as Moses had an encounter with the Living God at the burning bush. God speaks to us through the Bible, and thus we call it the "Word of God," for that is what it is.

**One Word—Many Versions.** A large number of "versions" of the Bible are available. So many, in fact, that it can be very confusing to the new convert or the unfamiliar. Since language is fluid and changes across the years, these versions have evolved primarily to make God's Word more readable and understandable for today's readers. Most of these versions are reliable translations from the original copies. It is important to understand, however, that some are paraphrases and not word- for- word translations. (Additional information regarding Bible versions can be found in the appendix)

There are many good books on how we got our Bible, and what makes it reliable and trustworthy. There are copious resources and aids for understanding the Bible. Many of the good study Bibles today have a wealth of information tucked between their covers, and there are many basic study tools such as Bible dictionaries, handbooks, commentaries and atlases. Any good Christian book store can expose you to these excellent resources. (Additional information regarding useful Bible aids can also be found in the appendix)

**Some Useful Tips for Studying God's Word.** *It is important to study the Bible itself.* Libraries could be filled with books written about the events, personalities, and truths of the Bible. They are helpful, but it is essential to study the primary source—the Bible itself. It is only then that study of the Bible becomes a real encounter with God.

*I must have a PLAN for my Bible study.* I should adopt some kind of systematic plan for Bible study. There are many plans, and in the beginning I may want to adopt one that has been proven and popular. I won't likely use the same plan year in and year out, or indefinitely, but using a systematic plan will keep my reading and study of the Bible from being spasmodic and haphazard.

*I must pray for the Holy Spirit to enlighten my reading—*Years ago, a visiting evangelist pointed out to me a beautiful prayer to preface all of my Bible reading with. It is Ps. 119:18, "Open my eyes that I may see wonderful things in your law." For many years I rarely opened the Bible without praying this prayer. God has richly rewarded my study of His Word. He has answered my prayer.

*One reading is not enough.* Another fundamental and practical suggestion for proper interpretation of the Bible is simply to *read a passage more than once.* Read it not just twice, but three or four times, or even a dozen times if necessary—and it will be necessary for some passages.

Years ago when I was teaching literature classes in high school, I challenged my students with this approach in regard to understanding the beauty and meaning of poetry. I recalled for them how novelist F. Scott Fitzgerald had said of "Ode on a Grecian Urn," by Keats, that he had read it perhaps 100 times before its full beauty and meaning touched him. Likewise, I must learn to "live" with some Scripture to absorb its richest meaning and power.

*I must approach my Bible study with the excitement of an explorer.* Oletta Wald, in her popular Bible study handbook, *The Joy of Discovery,* quotes William Barclay, "It is only when truth is discovered that it is appropriated. When a man is simply told the truth, it remains external to him and he can quite easily forget it. When he is led to discover the truth himself it becomes an integral part of him and he never forgets."[6]

Although Bible software programs can be an enormous help, they also pose some risks. Douglas Groothuis reminds us that "informational retrieval is not synonymous with handling the truth wisely . . . users may end up dissecting the Bible into info-chunks instead of understanding the Scripture's context, historical setting, and overall theological significance."[7]

*Some truth can only be discovered by the born-again believer.* R. A. Torrey believed that one who wishes to study the Bible profitably needs to be a "born-again" believer, needs to possess a willingness to work hard to understand its truths, and must have a willing heart to obey the truth God reveals. He also said, "you must come to Christ like a child to be taught what to believe and do, rather than coming as a full-grown person who already knows it all and must find some interpretation of Christ's words that will fit into your mature and infallible philosophy."[8]

Torrey also proposed a prayer one might profitably pray when beginning his or her Bible study: "Oh, God, make me a little child. Empty me of my own notions. Teach me Your own mind. Make me ready like a little child to receive all that You have to say, no matter how contrary it is to what I have thought before."[9]

Again the Navigator's *Bible Studies Handbook* states it well: "If you will study God's Word faithfully, pray for understanding, and diligently apply the Scriptures to your experience and daily walk, your life will change and increasingly glorify God."[10] If I am to follow Jesus faithfully, I must follow His *Blueprint* and build my Christian life according to code.

**THERE IS THE DISCIPLINE OF WHAT OTHERS HAVE WRITTEN.** Nothing can substitute for reading and studying the written Word of God. It is our Daily Bread. Jesus said, "Man does not live on bread alone, but on every word that comes from the mouth of God" (Mt. 4:4).

Nothing can feed the soul and spirit of man like God's own truth. It becomes not only the "measuring stick" for our own lives and conduct, but also for what others say and write. Obviously the world is full of books. Many of them, perhaps the majority of them, do not rank very highly when evaluated by God's measuring line of value, but many books are extremely valuable to us in recording, defining, and interpreting life.

Through the centuries Christian believers have written of their experiences in following Christ. Many devout and serious disciples have journaled and recorded not only their own experiences, but the experiences of other great souls. Many scholars and students of the Word and of the Christian faith have written down the results of their studies.

How impoverished would the world be, for instance, without the writings of St. Augustine, Francis of Assisi, Thomas A Kempis, Martin Luther, John Calvin, John Wesley, Andrew Murray, Oswald Chambers, C. S. Lewis, A. W. Tozer, Francis Schaeffer, and hundreds of others.

The great volume of Christian writings out there should be tantalizingly tempting to the serious follower of Christ. To neglect either the Bible itself, or the writings of our "trailblazing" brothers and sisters in Christ, is to risk either poverty or loss of soul.

The concern of the author is that far too few of today's Christians are *readers*. We are an age that has been raised with television, VCR's and now computers and video and computer games. While great learning can take place through these media, one wonders how interactive the mind and heart will be in the pursuit of Christian truth through these avenues?

A list of some of the Christian "classics," and contemporary works of repute will be provided in the appendix. It is the hope that those reading this book will develop a plan of reading from this list, or a similar one.

**THERE IS THE DISCIPLINE OF PRAYER.** Prayer is God's USB—His "universal connecting device" between our souls and the divine God. Or perhaps I might prefer to think of the privilege of prayer as an "internal modem" for easy access to the throne, and I won't need AOL, Compuserve, or any other ISP to get connected.

Prayer is talking to and listening to God. Can you picture a romantic courtship with little or no dialogue—a relationship between a husband and wife that does not involve conversation—both *listening* and *talking*?

As a pastor I have counseled with and observed some couples and marriages where very little authentic and meaningful conversation appeared to be happening. A marriage is unlikely to survive such a condition indefinitely. Indeed it is unlikely that any quality relationship can exist without good communication.

**A Vital Conversation with Our Divine Lover.** God has planned for a quality love relationship with every person. Prayer is the vital communication link with our divine Lover. When two people love each other, communication is generally not difficult. It is natural—as natural as breathing. And the love I feel for the One who showed great mercy to me and forgave my sins, makes it easy for me to want to thank Him and to express my love for Him.

That I need His continued mercy, strength, and help in my journey with Him is ever more obvious to me, even after years of walking with Him. This awareness in itself encourages my frequent conversations with my heavenly Lover, and helps to keep those conversations fresh. Mother Teresa says, "if we want to be able to love, we must be able to pray."[11]

But, if we find it difficult to imagine loving relationships without conversation, we do not fail to recognize that the pressures, responsibilities, and stresses of life can intrude mercilessly into our agendas and can crowd out or seriously affect this vital link with our God.

Wesley Duewel has written: "The greatest privilege God gives to you is the freedom to approach Him (God) at any time. You are not only authorized to speak to Him; you are invited . . . as a child of God you have full authority to contact God, the Sovereign of the universe. . . . God is never too busy to listen to you; He is never too involved to answer you."[12]

**Prayer Produces Results.** Someone has said that if there could be any "tears" in heaven, and God has already said there won't be, they would be shed over learning how great the power of prayer would have been had we really exercised it. Prayer can do anything that God can do. Jesus said, "Ask and it will be given to you, seek and you will find; knock and the door will be opened" (Mt. 7:7–8). Again, Jesus said, "And I will do whatever you ask in my name, so that the Son may bring glory to the Father" (Jn. 14:13).

Prayer opens up a "menu" window on our spiritual screen. God is asking, "What do you want me to do for you?"

Wesley Duewel says, "Prayer is the master strategy that God gives for the defeat and rout of Satan."[13] Jesus has planned for each of his disciples to be partners with Him in reaching a lost world. Duewel writes, "Prayer is the greatest resource of the church. . . . You yourself can influence more people for God and have a greater role in advancing Christ's cause by prayer than in any other way. It is not the *only* thing that you must do, but it is the *greatest* thing you can do. It has often been said,, 'The devil trembles when he sees/God's weakest child upon his knees.'"[14]

"William Wilberforce was the leader in the great British crusade to abolish the slave trade. Historians tell us that he and his colleagues, in a little circle called the Clapham sect, immersed their political strategizing and lobbying in daily three-hour sessions of intercessory prayer."[15]

Does this mean that one must pray three hours a day? No, but it does demonstrate the power of prayer against incredible odds. Ron Sider writes: "one of the greatest reasons for hope today is the powerful movements of prayer that are sweeping through the worldwide church. If large numbers of Christians rediscover the power of prayer and open themselves fully to the blessed Holy Spirit, God will make the next century a time of evangelistic explosion and social transformation."[16]

The anonymous writer, in the classic, *The Kneeling Christian*, asks, "Why are many Christians so often defeated? Because they pray so little. Why are many church-workers so often discouraged and disheartened? Because they pray so little. Why do most men see so few brought 'out of darkness into light' by their ministry? Because they pray so little. Why are not our churches simply on fire for God? Because there is so little real prayer. . . . *We may be assured of this—the secret of all failure is our failure in secret prayer.*"[17]

**My Secret Is Simple—I Pray.** An interviewer once said to Mother Teresa, "Mother Teresa, you love people whom others regard as human debris. What is your answer?" Mother Teresa replied, "My secret is simple. I pray." Through prayer, Mother Teresa "became the embodiment of inexhaustible compassion. She incarnated mercy across all barriers of race, color, and creed, and even beyond the boundaries of politics, ideologies, and nations . . . even governments were disarmed by the purity of Mother Teresa's approach to human beings and their needs. 'There is no one,' she said, 'who needs God's grace and help more than I do. I think that is why He uses me, because I cannot claim any credit for what gets done.'"[18]

**Useful Tips for Making Prayer Vital.** Let me suggest a few basic steps for developing power and perseverance through prayer:

(1) *I must bring love into my prayer life.* My conversations with God must be the conversations of love. Lovers do not find it hard to talk with one another. If discipline is there, it is a "delightful discipline," remembering as Oswald Chambers reminds us that prayer is not what it costs us to pray, but what it cost the Son of God to make it possible for us to pray.

(2) *My conversations must be simple and direct.* Prayer is my spiritual "dialog box," and I won't need to use HTML (hyper-text markings language) with God. When talking with God, one does not need a special kind of language— one sprinkled with *Thee's, Thou's, and Thines*, or words heavy with high-church terminology. God wants us to "see it big but keep it simple." We can talk to God just like we would talk to our lover.

(3) *I begin my conversations of love with adoration.* The Bible says God inhabits the praises of His people. There is no better way to begin to feel God's presence than to enter His

courts with praise. Tell God you love Him. Be creative in finding ways to express your love for your Divine Lover. A poet once wrote, "How do I love you/Let me count the ways." Perhaps you have quoted that to your spouse or sweetheart. C. Welton Gaddy said, "one day with a prayerful desire to express my love for God in specifics, I took a pen and sheet of paper and began to write:

I Love Your creativity—the way You can fill an
Ordinary day with momentous experiences;
Your ability to turn a bad situation into
An occasion for growth;
Your mercy which transforms
Episodes of sin into encounters with salvation.

I love your affinity for beauty.
I love your sense of humor.
I Love your steadfast presence.
I love Your vulnerability.
I love Your comfort.
I love Your commitment to community.
I love Your favor for underdogs.
I love Your passion for ministry, for peace
And for revelation.
I Love What you do and who You are.
I love you for being You, God![19]

You get the idea. I can personalize my love for God with my own pen and paper.

A common practice is to bring into your prayer time two books—the Bible and a hymnbook. I have often begun my prayer time quietly singing or humming the words of a hymn or chorus. "No exercise," says Jack Taylor, "will result in more healing physically, mentally, emotionally, and spiritually, than that of studying and practicing praise."[20] Nothing can prepare the heart for communion with God better than worship and praise which are always a "language of love."

(4) *I must schedule time for my Love Conversations.* The enemy of our souls will try to wreck our love relationship with God. One of his prime strategies for doing so is to steal my time with God. I must therefore *schedule* time with the One I love. It must be a high priority on my agenda. So, how often should I pray?

Gaddy says, "Lovers do not ask how often they should speak or seek to be together. The love they share renders that question meaningless. They know the joy in communion with each other; they prize constant contact, unbroken fellowship, and continuous communication. To commune with God means to live in love—to interact with the Ultimate Lover . . . an invitation to the wonder and joy of an unending love affair."[21]

Real love produces some extravagances—some excesses, like Mary's alabaster offering. David Ford says our intimacy with God will do the same. He says that sometimes that extravagance might just be "praying as long as it takes." He writes: "From time to time (probably best not regularly) when we go into our room, shut the door, and pray in secret, it is a good idea to allow God as long as God wants. How long is that? Who knows? But it would be surprising if a God of such abundance, who longs to communicate in love, could be satisfied with brief set times. It is easy to find ourselves treating God less generously than we treat our best friend, our spouse, or even our customers."[22]

I like to devote my dawns to God. All through the Bible, God desires and requires the *first* and *best* of sacrifices. It is amazing how complex and cluttered our day becomes as it wears on. Why not, therefore, give God time in the freshness of each day's dawn? Not everyone is a "morning person," of course, so whatever time you choose, it should be a prime time, a private time, and a practical time for intimate, personal communion with God.

(5) *Remember, lovers have no secrets.* God wants you to tell Him everything. Think how it is between young lovers. As Gaddy suggests, "Love affairs thrive on specifics. . . . Each lover wants the other to detail activities. 'Tell me about your day— tell me everything' 'I want to know how you really feel about what's going on.' 'What is bothering you?' 'Please let me know how I can best show you how much I love you.' Gaddy points out that "regular conversations about specific matters nurture communion between lovers."[23] *My Divine Lover is interested in the details of my life and how I feel. Tell Him everything.*

Then, it is important to remember that with lovers, *conversations are confidential and safe.* Gaddy says, "I can bare my soul with the confidence that nothing I say will cause God to stop loving me or deny me the joy of forgiveness and redemption."[24] Because of this, my prayer time can, and indeed must, include *confession.* There is no Christian, now or ever, who hasn't failed God or sinned. No wonder Jesus taught us to pray, "Forgive us our debts as we forgive our debtors."

The Psalmist prayed, "May the words of my mouth, and the meditation of my heart be pleasing in your sight . . ." (Ps. 19:14). Interestingly enough, that's about as far as most of us need to go in allowing God to search our hearts and lives. What have I been saying? Have my words been negative, critical, or hurtful? What have I been meditating upon? What has occupied my thoughts—material concerns or spiritual matters? Evil reports or good reports?

This is probably the toughest part of prayer—admitting that we have failed or sinned and asking God's forgiveness. It is hard on our pride, but it must be done, and Jesus promised, "If we confess our sins, He is faithful and just, and will forgive us our sins and purify us from all unrighteousness" (1 Jn. 1:9).

Catherine of Genoa's prayer of confession was filled with the hope and love that should characterize this aspect of prayer. She said, "I've been abysmally wrong, and I grieve for that. . . . But my world is bright, for I am surrounded and embraced by limitless love. The past is over. I will go now where love leads me."[25]

(6) *My prayers must not get stuck on myself.* "Others" is a good word to tuck into your prayer vocabulary. The first words of the prayer our Lord taught us to pray, *"Our Father,"* lets us know that we not only have a Heavenly Father, but there are more in this family than *me*. We need to pray for others in the church family and in our homes. Can we imagine what would happen in our homes if there was more prayer and less hassling of one another?

Want to know who else to pray for? I can start with those with whom I find it difficult to relate? I can pray for those in authority in the church, in the city, in the state, and in our nation and the world. Paul said, "I urge . . . first of all, that requests, prayers, intercessions, and thanksgiving be made for everyone; for kings, and for all those in authority . . ." (1 Tim. 2:1).

Pray for a passion for souls. Pray for revival and a worldwide spiritual awakening. There is so much to pray for.

(7) *I must claim victory for my prayer life through faith.* I must refuse to allow Satan to bully me in this crucial area of my spiritual life. As surely as Jesus saved me from sin, He can save me from an impotent and unmeaningful prayer life.

Satan will make insidious assaults upon us during and following our prayer times. I must have strong faith that God has heard my prayers. I must leave everything in His hands with the quiet confidence that He will do what I cannot do and will empower me to do what I must do.

Gaddy writes: "Persistent prayer requires discipline, as do love and love affairs. However, the discipline of prayer (and of love) is not an act of confinement or punishment, but an invitation to intimacy, freedom, and unparalleled joy."[26]

**OTHER CLASSIC DISCIPLINES FOR SERIOUS FOLLOWERS.** There are many other disciplines that have characterized Christian disciples across the ages. Dallas Willard groups the principal disciplines as 1) disciplines of *abstinence*: solitude, silence, fasting, frugality, chastity, secrecy, and sacrifice, and 2) disciplines of *engagement*: study, worship, celebration, service, prayer, fellowship, confession and submission.[27]

Others might group them differently, and add or subtract other disciplines. A disciple will want to be familiar with all of these and employ such additional disciplines as the Lord may direct at specific junctures of one's spiritual journey. Richard Foster begins his well-known book, *Celebration of Discipline*, saying, "Superficiality is the curse of our age. The doctrine of instant satisfaction is a primary spiritual problem."[28]

Indeed superficiality characterizes most aspects of life today, both secular and spiritual, but it is especially devastating to Christian life and witness. Foster says, "The classical disciplines of the spiritual life call us to move beyond surface living into the depths . . . they urge us to be the answer to a hollow world."[29]

# WILL I BE A DISCIPLE OR A CHRISTAHOLIC?

Calvin Miller says, "many Christians are only 'Christaholics' and not disciples at all. Disciples are cross-bearers; they seek Christ. Christaholics seek happiness. Disciples dare to discipline themselves, and the demands they place on themselves leave them enjoying the happiness of their growth. Christaholics are escapists looking for a shortcut to nirvana. Like drug addicts, they are trying to 'bomb out' of their depressing world. There is no automatic joy. Christ is not a happiness capsule; he is the way to the Father. But the way to the Father is not a carnival ride in which we sit and do nothing while we are whisked through various spiritual sensations."[30]

In the eighteenth century, John Wesley said: "It was a common saying among the Christians of the primitive church, 'the soul and the body make a man; the spirit and discipline make a Christian; implying that none could be a real Christian without the help of Christian discipline. But if this be so, is it any wonder that we find so few Christians; for where is Christian discipline?"[31] I doubt Wesley would be more encouraged by what he would find today.

Richard Taylor says, "Discipline is what moderns need the most and want the least."[32] and Dallas Willard says that "people whom we acknowledge to be far superior to us—and in the case of Jesus Himself, even divine—found it necessary to practice the disciplines and engage in activities with which we blithely dismiss . . . and he asks, "What leads us to believe that we might be an exception to the rule and might know the power of the kingdom life without the appropriate discipline? How could we be justified in doing anything less than practicing and teaching the disciplines Jesus Christ himself and the best of his followers found necessary?"[33]

Willard calls for the Christian community to place the spiritual disciplines at the heart of the gospel—"to remove the disciplines from the category of historical curiosities and place them at the center of the new life in Christ . . ." He says, "this is an age for spiritual heroes—a time for men and women to be heroic in faith and in spiritual character and power . . . holiness and devotion must come forth from the closet and the chapel to possess the street and the factory, the schoolroom and boardroom, the scientific laboratory and the governmental office."[34]

And perhaps Philip Yancey says it best: "I persevere at spiritual disciplines no matter how I feel. I do this for one main goal, the goal of all spiritual discipline: I want to know God more fully."[35] That indeed must be the heart of all our discipleship.

"The spirit of the disciplines," says Willard, "is nothing but the love of Jesus, with its resolute will to be like him whom we love."[36]

Though none can be disciples without discipline, it is also questionable whether any can be disciples in isolation. In the next chapter we will discover the importance of finding fellow travelers for our spiritual journey.

# QUESTIONS FOR REFLECTION

1.   Have I really thought about how I can be a good steward of God's gift of forgiveness and the privilege of following Him?

2.   Am I willing to seriously train and discipline myself for my journey of discipleship?

3.   How well do I know God's master blueprint for my life? Am I willing to study that blueprint diligently?

4.   What aids to understanding the Bible do I have on hand? What others am I willing to acquire?

5. Are my prayers natural and intimate, or are they forced, unnatural, and ineffective?

6. Do my prayers employ joyful praise as well as petitions?

7. Am I willing to learn from other historical and contemporary followers of Jesus? Do I read books and magazines that highlight Christian lifestyle and experience?

8. Name at least five other classical spiritual disciplines besides prayer and Bible study.

9. Why did Philip Yancey say he persisted in the disciplines?

10. Honestly, what part does discipline play in *MY* journey?

---

## A PRAYER FOR SERIOUS FOLLOWERS

Father, I know that I am saved and kept by your grace through faith in Jesus Christ. Still, I know that you will never violate my free will. I know that I must choose to be a good steward of my natural gifts and abilities, and of the gifts of the Spirit just as I chose to receive your Son as my Savior.

As your disciple, I dare not discount the value of *discipline*. Help me to learn from your Word, from the experience of other disciples, and from cultivating deep, intimate conversations with You.

Let me not be a "spiritual sprinter," but a "marathon runner." I mean to finish this race. I know that conversion is a miracle of a moment, but I also realize that it takes a lifetime to make a saint. Let me be a life-long learner. In Jesus' name, Amen.

# CHAPTER SEVEN

# CAN I MAKE IT ON MY OWN?

*Commitment will not be effective unless it finds expression in a committed fellowship. If we have any knowledge of human nature, we begin by rejecting the arrogance of self-sufficiency.*

—Elton Trueblood

*We cannot have general cultural recovery without a burning faith, and faith will not be revived except through redemptive fellowships which serve to crack open even the most hostile world.*

—Elton Trueblood

Among the many paradoxes of this Christian faith is the irony that while the gospel makes "individuals" out of every one of us, it does not leave us *alone*. Indeed it is unlikely that a Christian believer can make it alone, or in isolation indefinitely.

David McKenna writes: "Few, if any of us are able to be at home in the presence of God as 'holy solitaires.' This was Wesley's term for those who assumed that they could grow without the body of Christ. We need communal discipline as the complement to our personal discipline . . ."[1]

## I Must Find Fellow Travelers for My Journey

Wesley also said, "It is a blessed thing to have fellow travelers to the New Jerusalem. If you do not find any, you must make them, for none can travel this road alone."[2]

If I am to develop individually as a Christian, I will need the help of other believers and disciples. That's where the *Church* comes into the picture. Christ is our supreme Master and mentor, but He meant for us to help one another in this journey. He didn't just call *one* person to be His disciple. He called *twelve*—twelve very ordinary, flesh and blood persons to pour His life and teachings into. He gave them specific instructions, tasks, and work to do.

And Christ gives today's disciples instructions, commands, tasks, and work to do—work that cannot be done alone, without Him or without the community of faith. Wesley Tracy writes interestingly about the giant Redwood trees in California. He says that with their endurance record across centuries, one would suppose that these trees had roots that penetrate deeply into the soil and wrap around huge boulders.

But Tracy enlightens us: "Actually, they have shallow roots . . . they grow in groves, and the roots of many trees entwine. They stand together against the storms as if to announce to the north wind, '*we stand together*. If you are going to take one of us out, you will have to take us all.'"[3]

The parallel is easy enough to see. Christ knew that I would need a "spiritual family" to nurture me, and to help train me. He knew I would need a "refuge" from the storms of life—just as children thrive better in their natural families as they grow up.

It is noteworthy that when Jesus appointed His twelve disciples, He called them "that they might be with Him and that He might send them out . . ." (Mk. 3:14). Involved here is both the "inward spiritual journey"—sitting at Jesus' feet and learning from Him, and the "outward journey"—putting what we absorb from Jesus into practice in our daily lives—in the "world" setting.

It is true for us as individual followers, but that is also the twin-edged purpose of the church. The church can help us to worship Christ and to know Him better. It can provide encouragement and support in our trials, and it also gives us a way to minister and serve others, both within the body of Christ and in the world of unbelievers.

The Western, and especially the American culture, has been a fiercely proud and independent one, which perhaps militates against the concept of Christianity as a "community affair," but I must resist that spirit if I would develop a robust spiritual maturity and become useful and fruitful for my Lord. A single lump of coal does not give off much heat. Coals heaped together feed off one another and can warm the world.

Again, Wesley Tracy points out that John Wesley realized this truth and called his religious movement a "connexion." "He worked hard and successfully to keep those early Wesleyans 'connected.' He created spiritual formation structures that included societies, classes, bands, one-to-one spiritual guidance, and a design for family religion."[4]

George Whitefield and John Wesley were both great evangelists in their day, but at the end of his life Whitefield looked back regretfully, saying, "Brother Wesley acted wisely. The souls that were awakened under his ministry, he joined in class, and thus preserved the fruits of his labor. This I neglected, and my people are a rope of sand."[5]

Most healthy churches today try to offer both larger group-type, or "congregational" worship experiences, and also the smaller, cell-type experience, which encourages inter-action. The goal of the traditional Sunday School, has always been to accomplish the latter, but today, in many churches the home-centered, week-day (or night) Bible studies are very popular and provide an opportunity to both learn and to accomplish outreach.

Ron Sider writes: "I am convinced that the sinful pressures of the larger society are so strong that it is nearly impossible to follow Jesus without close, regular Christian fellowship. In our crazy society it is *very hard* to resist advertisers' alluring materialism, and Hollywood's seductive sexual nonsense. We need daily prayer, regular encouragement, and honest challenge of trusted sisters and brothers to live like Jesus."[6]

The high-tech world of television and computers comprises risks as well as promise. Douglas Groothuis cautions: "The fast paced, image dominated and driven nature of television renders intellectual reflection almost impossible . . . countless hours of peering at entertaining images dulls one's apprehension of the real world and *erodes the sense of community between human beings who are worthy of respect*."[7]

Regarding the so-called *virtual community*, created by computers, Groothuis quotes David Wells with this warning: "Our computers are starting to talk to us while our neighbors are becoming more distant and anonymous," and Groothuis adds, "I may 'connect' with terminals around the globe but know nothing of the pains, joys, and mundanities of the soul next door."[8]

Jesus probably expects twenty-first century disciples to make use of the technologies available, but He also insists that we develop and maintain meaningful relationships in real communities both inside and outside of the Church.

## What Can the Church Provide?

In my journey of discipleship, the church can provide me, a third millennium Christian, just what it provided the first-century apostles and the disciples down through the first 2,000 years of church history.

We read in *Acts*, that the early disciples "devoted themselves to the apostles' teaching and to fellowship, to the breaking of bread and to prayer . . . they broke bread together with glad and sincere hearts, praising God and enjoying favor of all the people. And the Lord added to their number daily those who were being saved" (Acts 2:42, 46–47).

In that cryptic account of the early church we see the dynamics of grace at work in the body of believers—the church. We see *unity* (all believers were together), *prayer* (corporate intercession), *mutual support for and care of one another* (they had everything in common—giving to anyone who had a need), *worship* (praising God), and *study* (the teaching of the apostles). Their "breaking of bread" not only was the sharing of regular meals, but the sharing of the Lord's Supper.

They were having a "spiritual feast" with one another, because Jesus was in their midst as He promised. There is always this spiritual feasting that takes place when and wherever the followers of Jesus meet together. It is a feast that the world knows nothing of and cannot imagine. It is the mystery of grace at work in the commonality of faith found in the individual believers.

I cannot afford to rob myself of this feast. The nature of "doing" church may change drastically in the third millennium, but a disciple of Jesus, whatever the century or age, will need other believers to worship with, to lean upon, to learn from, and to link arms with in order not only to fulfill the mission Christ gave to the church, but also to keep the inner fire of faith burning brightly in one's own soul.

## How Do I Find the "Right" Church?

I may already have a "church home." Perhaps it is the church that I attended as a child, or was introduced to by a friend. That church may exhibit the qualities identified in the New Testament church as described in the Acts of the Apostles and in the epistles. It may be a church that is meeting my needs, providing accountability and opportunities to serve.

On the other hand, whether I have only recently become a Christian, or am just now discovering the need for a closer following of Jesus, I may wonder, "how does one go about finding a proper church home?" In a society that is saturated with many denominations, independent churches, sects, and para-church groups, how do I know that I am choosing an authentic expression of the body of Christ?

Obviously it is beyond the scope and purpose of this book to cover this subject extensively, but if it is essential that followers and disciples of Jesus find a group of believers to meld with, it is also important that care be given to that process. At least three things are important in choosing a church. Consider: 1) What a church believes, 2) What a church *is*, and, 3) What a church *does*.

## What a Church Believes

Perhaps nothing is more important than "what a church believes." In time past, no one would consider choosing a church on any other ground than "What do these people *believe*?" But the times have changed. People are choosing their churches, not on the basis of doctrine, but whether this or that church has good music, an exciting children's program or activities, whether the services make me *feel good* about myself, or are meeting my "felt needs."

Often choosing a church to attend is given no greater thought or preference than a family might give in selecting a fast food restaurant for the day. Who is offering the best "special" of the day? What celebrity Christian singer is appearing? Or, well, let's see, what are my tastes for the day?

Candidly, music, children's ministry and worship experiences are all important, and people do expect quality, but none of these factors should overshadow what a church *believes* and is *teaching*. What we believe affects how we live. Our lifestyle is governed by what we hold as *truth*.

It is essential that I know what a particular body of believers hold as their articles of faith or their basic doctrines about God, about Jesus Christ, about the Holy Spirit. Do they believe in the Trinity?

I must investigate what the church teaches about the Holy Scriptures. Do they believe that the 66 books of the Old and New Testaments were given by divine inspiration, inerrantly revealing the will of God concerning us in all things necessary to our salvation? What does this church teach about "original sin"? About repentance? About baptism? About the second coming of Christ? About heaven and hell? About the church itself?

Generally, these beliefs will be found in written form and called articles of faith, church doctrine, constitution, or some other appropriately identifying name. One should not be timid about asking to read a copy of what the church believes, and should read it very carefully and ask questions if need be.

Church researchers and experts tell us that in the new millennium many will be trying to "mix and match" beliefs and create their own systems of synthetic faiths and religions. Perhaps the most serious challenge of all will be the confrontation with postmodernism which teaches that there is no *absolute truth*—that "truth" is only a "social construct" that can mean whatever a particular group of people want it to mean to accomplish their particular aims and goals.

Perhaps no one has seen the importance of *truth* and its consequences to all of life better than the eminent theologian/philosopher, Francis Schaeffer. In *A Christian Manifesto,* Schaeffer points out that we got where we are in modern culture and society morally and spiritually because of our basic view of reality. He says, "our view of final reality—whether it is material-energy, shaped by impersonal chance, or the living God and Creator—will determine our position on every crucial issue we face today. It will determine our views on the value and dignity of people, the base for the kind of life the individual and society lives, the direction law will take, and whether there will be freedom or some form of authoritarian dominance."[9] The point here is that our religious beliefs cannot be irrelevant. What we believe will ultimately affect how we live. How we live affects our society and our world. God gave us His Word to help guide us into truth. We cannot afford to build our lives on error.

Discovering what is truth in regard to finding the "right" church, can be a daunting experience for the uninformed, new Christian. But there are those who can help. It is important to test a church's beliefs with mainstream orthodox Christianity. The universal church cuts across denominational lines and has a rich history and tradition. It is important to weigh church beliefs by the body of truth that has characterized the mainstream church through the centuries.

In this work, we cannot examine in depth the basic theological beliefs of the Church. However, while the essential beliefs of the Christian faith may be worded in different ways and expressed in more expansive forms, the following brief statements touch the heart of what the author believes the Bible to declare:

1. There is One God—The Father, Son, and Holy Spirit, constituting the Holy Trinity.

2. The Holy Bible, containing the Old and New Testament Scriptures, is given by plenary inspiration, and contains all truth necessary to faith and Christian living.

3. Man is born in sin, and in his unregenerate state is inclined to evil and that continually.

4. The Atonement through Jesus Christ is for the whole human race, and whoever repents and believes on the Lord Jesus Christ is justified and regenerated and saved from the dominion of sin.

5. Believers are to be filled with The Holy Spirit and sanctified wholly through faith in the Lord Jesus Christ, and are to walk in the Spirit.

6. The Holy Spirit bears witness to the work that He does in the human heart and life.

7. Jesus Christ, Our Lord, will return to earth, the dead shall be raised, and the final judgment take place. Heaven and a glorious everlasting life will be the reward of those who are saved and obediently follow Jesus in discipleship.

8. Those who are finally unrepentant are hopelessly lost, and will suffer eternally in hell.

The Wesleyan quadrilateral—Scripture, reason, tradition, and experience—provides a proper paradigm balance for those seeking to evaluate, not only a church's beliefs but the total picture.

## What a Church Is?

In seeking out a body of believers to be my fellow travelers in my spiritual journey through this life, it is not only important to be enlightened as to what the beliefs are, but to have a feel for whether those particular beliefs are being effectively fleshed out in the lives of these people that I'm considering making my spiritual soul-mates. Another way to put it is are these people "walking their talk"?

Now obviously, we can't get into *judging* here, (more about that under, "Can I Find That Perfect Church?") but one will have a feel about whether the Holy Spirit is at work in this body of believers. Is there a polar cap on the pulpit and icicles hanging off the church pews, so to speak? Is there a fair amount of love being demonstrated among these folks? Is there kindness and compassion expressed between members and toward the unsaved? Is there an expression of genuine joy and praise manifested in the worship of God? Do the folks in this church seem to be genuine in regard to their faith and in all areas of their lives?

George Barna suggests that today one of the first factors people will search for is "are these people 'real' and can they be trusted, or is it simply a religious ritual, a social game they play?" Perhaps people have never needed secure, caring relationships more than today. Barna says, "as traditional marriage and networks collapse, loneliness will become epidemic and the church must be ready to meet that need."[10]

## What a Church Does?

Obviously a church does many things. Sometimes too many things. Expectations for churches have never been greater. Many want the church to provide services that stretch the church beyond its resources and abilities. And often, churches have no clear idea about what they should be doing, or what is their priority of mission. It is necessary that we think clearly about what a church should be doing—what its core mission should be.

Clearly, if we are going to follow the biblical pattern, we discover some distinctive mandates and patterns in the New Testament church. Going back to our earlier Scripture, Mark 3:14, as well as the study of Acts 2:42–47, we find that the twin-edged mission of the church was to 1) to gather around Jesus in worship and learning, and, then, 2) to take His truth to the world.

One can hardly improve upon that as the purpose of the church in a nutshell. That is a framework upon which all else hangs. Of course that is like the "rough-in carpentry," in building a house, and there is a lot of "finish work" to be done. But the mission of the church should be centered upon worshiping Jesus, exalting

Him, and learning from Him, and then taking His truth and the gospel to the world.

Again, there are multitudes of ways of "gathering people" around Jesus, worshiping Him and learning about Him, but it must be done. Likewise, there are hundreds of ways of proclaiming God's love and truth to the unsaved and unchurched, but it must be done, and it must be a high priority. Most church leaders would say that in one way or another every program or ministry in the church should be related to or have as its bottom line the purpose of winning people to Jesus and making disciples of them (Mt. 28:19, 20). It is what Stephen Covey would call, "keeping the main thing the main thing."

Elton Trueblood reminds us that "the church is never true to itself when it is living for itself, for if it is chiefly concerned with saving its own life, it will lose it. The nature of the Church is such that it must always be engaged in finding new ways by which to transcend itself. Its main responsibility is always outside its own walls in the redemption of common life."[11]

Choosing a church home can be confusing in these postmodern times when there is so much syncretism and synthetic religion, and so many cults around. And no doubt there are other important criteria to help one in making that choice. Certainly, that decision should not be made lightly or impulsively, and it should be bathed in a generous amount of prayer.

It is also important to keep in mind that the *true church* is made up of all those who have been born again by the Spirit of God. That body of believers cuts across denominational lines, and no one church can claim to be the *one and only true church*.

C. William Fisher once wrote, "How absurd it must seem . . . to see so many professing Christians, especially the professionals, standing around this artesian well of living water, each saying, 'yes, the Fountain of Spiritual Life is flowing freely—but the water will do you no good unless you drink it out of my cup.'" Fisher continues, saying, "The good news is that the Living Water will slake the thirst and satisfy the parched soul no matter whose cup is used."[12]

In the following chapter we will discuss two potential perils in relation to finding a church home and enjoying it: expecting to find a perfect church, and the threat of spectatorism.

## QUESTIONS FOR REFLECTION

1. Why is "independent" or "solitaire" discipleship difficult, if not an oxymoron?

2. How can a "spiritual family" make my journey of discipleship easier and more fruitful?

3. Why did evangelist, George Whitefield, call his converts a "rope of sand"?

4. Name three things a believer should consider in finding the "right" church home?

5. Why do people increasingly need to find loving and secure relationships in their spiritual families today?

6. Does the main responsibility of a church lie *within* or outside its walls?

# A PRAYER FOR SERIOUS FOLLOWERS

Dear Jesus, I know that I can't make it alone in this journey of discipleship. I, too, must find fellow travelers. In order to mature in the faith, I know that I will need communal discipline and accountability as well as personal discipline.

I pray for Your guidance in finding my "spiritual family." Help me to find a body of believers who believe right, live right, love deep and long, and are making a difference in their culture.

And, Jesus, help me not to expect more out of these fellow travelers than I should, but may we all reflect the "imago Christi," and help to shake our world with your love. In Jesus Name, Amen.

# CHAPTER EIGHT

# CAN I FIND THAT PERFECT CHURCH?

*By this all men will know that you are my disciples, if you have love for one another.*

—Jesus

*It is in community that we learn who our neighbor is. Community is the true school of love.*

—Henri Nouwen

*We have a sinful self to be crucified with Christ, a human self to be controlled by Christ, in order that the true self may be realized in Christ.*

—W. T. Purkiser

Many folks drift from one church or denomination to another searching for a perfect church climate, where the winds of differing opinion never rise, and the sea of human relationships is never disturbed. Often, too, people hope that all their personal tastes in worship, education, and fellowship will be catered to. They forget that they are only *one*.

The church is composed of many individuals. We are all inter-connected through Christ, but each person displays his or her own distinctive "web-page"—revealing unique gifts, personalities, temperaments, etc. And even the individual's tastes and moods change or vary from time to time. No church could possibly satisfy every individual equally all of the time.

Edith Schaeffer, in her book *What is a Family?*, wrote something about the family that is equally true of the church. She said, "People throw away what they could have, by insisting on perfection which they cannot have, and looking for it where they will never find it."[1]

## Redeemed, but Not Perfect

The church is composed of imperfect human beings. Admittedly, it ought to be a constituency of *redeemed* human beings whose lives and conduct are characterized by love, understanding, and patience, and whose attitudes and conduct are Spirit-controlled, magnifying Jesus. Nevertheless, there will never be a church body that does not evidence ample amounts of humanity, notwithstanding the holiness of its people. Holiness does not cancel our humanity, but it should help us to discipline and control it.

Do I understand that people's moods fluctuate? Some people do not wander from church to church, but they oscillate between highs and lows. They live from one church crisis to another. It would almost seem that they thrive when they can be involved in some church conflict or difficulty. In point of fact however, they forfeit not only their own peace, but often inflict terrible damage upon the church, while pampering their own moods.

When I become a part of a "church family," I have a personal responsibility to contribute to its health and well-being. I need to accept the fact that there will be internal conflicts from time to time. It is how the church family solves those conflicts that will bear testimony of the quality of love found here.

Again, Edith Schaeffer, in speaking of the home, says, "There is a beauty and continuity which can never be had unless someone in the family has the certainty that the whole art form (home or family unit) is more important than one incident, or even string of incidents."[2]

How true this is of the church also. Church members must be convinced that the church as a whole, is more important than any single issue or problem, or even string of problems. Without such a conviction, and without a deep commitment to the church's total life and witness, issues can divide the church, weaken its witness, and nullify its message.

## We Must Not "Nurse" Our Hurts

I must remember that *people* are always more important than programs, but I must also understand that no one in the community of believers is permitted the luxury of nursing a personal injury or hurt along to make it a divisive church issue. Very few issues in the church are "life and death" issues. There are a few, but I must be very selective over what I am willing to spill my blood or the blood of my brothers and sisters in Christ over.

The Christian way is not to brood over personal injuries, imagined or real, but to give them to Jesus Christ. I must be quick to forgive and quick to forget. I must let Jesus purge my attitudes, and I must seek to be an effective part of the "healing ministry" and "blessing potential" of the church.

Our youngest son and his wife have four children. They have a "word" for the child who feels he or she has been wounded, fairly or unfairly, and whines too long about it. The word is "get over it." That may seem cold and heartless, but it is not when put within the framework of a home where there are ample amounts of love, security, and discipline. It would be more heartless to let a child grow up believing that if they wallow in self-pity long enough over life's injustices they will finally be vindicated and get their own way.

The writer of Hebrews said, "make every effort to live in peace with all men and to be holy; without holiness no one will see the Lord. See to it that no one misses the grace of God and that no bitter root grows up to cause trouble and defile many" (Heb. 12:14, 15).

Just as the natural family serves as a microcosm of "life at large," where we learn how to live together, to love one another, and to work out our problems, so the church family is also a microcosm where Christian believers learn to live out their faith and test their love on one another, while exalting Christ and fulfilling the Great Commission. If that scene is not too attractive to the world, then the unchurched world has a right to say, "Physician heal thyself."

## Abandonment Does Not "Fix" Families or Churches

Today, *abandonment* is a ready option for those seeking to escape from facing their misunderstandings, problems, or even their sins. Sometimes people are willing to trample on their vows for their own selfish pursuits or goals, or what they think are their *rights*. This is true of our natural families and of the church family.

Once, these institutions were considered worth preserving. People who laid vows upon themselves before a church altar, were committed to keeping those vows and sticking with their spouses or their churches. They were not looking for an escape, nor would they seriously consider abandonment except as a *last resort*.

I hear people say, "I love my church, but I just cannot attend there as long as______. (You fill in the blank). But that is a hard thing for me to get hold of. If something is broken, how do you fix it? Surely not by abandoning it? Edith Schaeffer says, "a terrible loneliness is ahead for people who have torn up their own homes with their own hands."[3] It is true of the church family also. There can be no celebration of broken vows.

Vows are easily broken today, and people try to go on living as celebrants, but there is no joy in broken vows. The mind distrusts it and rebels. The heart forbids it. The "wine of grace" is never served at the *breaking* of vows, only in the *keeping* of them. There is no intoxication of joy when vows are broken, only death.

Something dies, but it is not the vows. Vows cannot be buried. No hearse can be found to carry off broken vows. No minister to officiate the burial. Trying to bury broken vows is like trying to bury the living. Despair may very well stalk the vow-breaker. Depression and darkness can converge like crows on their prey.

If this seems like too dark of a picture I am painting, we must realize that the Lord intended that families and churches be bathed in divine love. He intended that our strong bonds and commitments to each other should provoke from the world words like "Behold how they love one another," and all too often our collective witness has shown just the opposite.

*Selfishness* is at the root of so much of the trouble in families and church relationships. Yet, isn't that precisely what *holiness* addresses? Isn't this the "ax laid at the root of the tree" (Mt. 3:10). Jesus taught, "If anyone would come after me, he must deny himself, and take up his cross and follow me" (Mt. 16:24). And Paul said, "I have been crucified with Christ, and I no longer live, but Christ lives in me" (Gal. 2:20).

These words from *God Calling*, by A. J. Russell, seem appropriate when there is trouble in the family: "Learn of me. Kill the self. Every blow to self is used to shape the real, eternal imperishable you. . . . Be very candid and rigorous with yourselves. 'Did *self* prompt that?' And if it did, oust it at all costs . . . it is not life and its difficulties you have to conquer, only the self in you."[4]

The Apostle Paul was careful to warn the New Testament church about the damage that can be caused through *disunity*. He wrote the Philippians: "I urge you to live a life worthy of the calling you have received. Be completely humble and gentle; be patient, bearing with one another in love. Make every effort to keep the unity of the Spirit through the bond of peace" (Phil. 4:1,2).

And to the Colossians, Paul said, "As God's chosen people, holy and dearly loved, clothe yourselves with compassion, kindness, humility, gentleness and patience. Bear with each other and forgive whatever grievances you may have against one another. Forgive as the Lord forgave you. And over all these virtues put on love, which binds them together in perfect unity" (Col. 3: 12–14).

Obviously the Lord knew that we would have to battle against discontent, dissension, and disunity in our families, our churches, and in our communal relationships, and the New Testament forthrightly addresses the problem.

Webster's definition of the words *to abandon* and its derivatives include: "to withdraw in the face of danger, to give up with the intent of never again claiming a right or interest in; to withdraw protection, support or help from; to desert; to forsake and to give up completely." I must confess that those words in the context of *relationships* frighten me terribly.

So what are the options to *abandonment*? Issues must be dealt with in conflict resolution, but never within the framework of *blame,* or with the agenda of "reforming" the other party. Try brokenness and asking and seeking forgiveness. Jesus said, "If you do not forgive men their sins, your Father will not forgive your sins" (Mt. 6:15).

Persons in conflict usually feel that "someone" isn't listening to them. A good starting point in resolving conflict, then, is to allow all parties to be fully heard in a non-judgmental setting. Effective communication can often help parties to realize that their goals are actually the same, or very similar, and with a bit of "give and take" with regard to methods, the conflict can be resolved.

Several things should be kept in mind in dealing with conflict. First, *persons* are more important than "programs." Care and compassion for *individuals* is a priority. Second, the health of the *institution* itself—be it a marriage, a family, or a church body—possesses great worth. Third, *affirmation* builds trust in relationships. Criticism of persons often breeds distrust and dissension. Fourth, resolving conflicts generally requires *time*. It has been said that 80 percent of compromise happens in the last 20 percent of time. That's a good reason to avoid hasty abandonment.

So, is there never a time to "leave" a church or a relationship? Undoubtedly there is, but *if* it must be done, let it be done only as a last resort—only after a compassionate and selfless effort at reconciliation, and only after a generous amount of prayer and time.

It is not possible to live in either our natural families or our church families without human relationship problems. Though redeemed, we are still human, but God expects that the marvelous grace He died to provide for us, will be applied at every point of irritation or failure. To run from those problems will only be to ride a moonless night with the witches.

Since we are concerned here with being "followers" and "disciples" of Christ, perhaps Willard's succinct assessment of church turmoil is right on target: "most problems in contemporary churches can be explained by the fact that members have not yet decided to follow Christ."[5]

The fantasy of expecting to find a "perfect church" is one peril the disciple must be prepared for, but there is another danger for the disciple in relation to the church—it is the threat of *spectatorism*.

## Can I Hang Loose and Be a Disciple?

When I have found "my spiritual family"—the church that I believe God has directed me to, there is not only the risk of being disappointed if I am expecting to find "that perfect church," but there is also the threat of yielding to the temptation toward *spectatorism*. The inclination to settle into a comfortable modality of non-involved observance will be enormous.

Former President John F. Kennedy was an early advocate for "fitness" in this country. In an address before the National Football Foundation, he once said, "Football today is far too much a sport for the few who can play it well; the rest of us, and too many of our children get our exercise from climbing up the seats in stadiums, or from walking across the room to turn on our television sets."[6] The remote control today has easily eliminated that last vestige of "exercise."

Spectatorism has its perils not only for physical fitness but also for spiritual well-being. It can cheapen Christianity. D. Elton Trueblood wrote: "Cheap Christianity can usually pull a pretty good attendance on Sunday morning. It is cheap whenever people think of themselves as spectators at a performance."[7]

If we would be disciples, we must understand that Jesus didn't say, "Come join the audience," but "take my yoke upon you." The yoke is the demands of discipleship.

It is following Jesus in very specific, practical, and concrete ways. Jesus called real flesh-and-blood disciples and welded them into a visible, organized church and gave them real jobs to do. He gave us the church not only to provide the mechanics, structure, and organization for evangelizing a lost world, but also to prevent our faith from remaining invisible and coldly abstract.

It is unlikely that one can love Christ and be devoted to Him, and not love His church and be devoted to it. When we fail to serve God through His church in concrete, self-sacrificing ways, our profession becomes bland and meaningless. After all, the church was made possible by love that expressed itself in very visible, concrete ways—like laying aside the splendor and comforts of heaven and coming to a smelly stable in this world; like hungering and thirsting, being misunderstood and rejected, and like bleeding and suffering on a rough-timbered cross and tasting death for thieves and taunters.

Oswald Chambers, in *Approved Unto God,* said, "God gives us marvelous hours of insight, then He withdraws them, and we have to begin to work out 'with aching hands and bleeding feet' what we saw in the vision, and few understand this."[8]

Great, inspiring services in themselves do not make a disciple out of one. That's why Jesus did not allow Peter to build his tabernacles at the corner of Mt. Transfiguration and Bright Cloud Boulevard.

The devil also has a "diversionary strategy" in today's culture. His plan is to get church families so absorbed in multiple activities: social events, children's athletic programs, gymnastic schedules, and trying to balance two work schedules, that juggling these things drains all of their energies and time so that very little is left for the church. Yet the church, next to the family itself, is probably the most important institution of all.

Satan is even sneakier. He often succeeds in getting church folks trailing off after quasi-religious activities. The "big sing" is the thing. The big convention gets the attention. Religious films and entertainment, Christian clubs and para-church groups gobble up the few available hours of weary church members.

Many of these things are not without value. They can conceivably strengthen and enrich believers, and indirectly, the church, if engaged selectively. But the real work of the church has never been done by "religious gadabouts," but by those who "stand in the gap." Spectatorism may help to cheer games on, but wars are won in the trenches by soldiers who make sacrifices, and I must realize that the battle against sin and Satan is not a game.

Phineas F. Bresee gave this caution to the young church he founded: He said there are those, "who run here and there wherever they hear the loudest firing . . . they are not the people who make circumstances and conditions and who bring things to pass. One soldier is worth a battalion of such." He continued, "I am deeply interested in the work of God everywhere. But I am absorbed with the battle God gave me to fight. . . . If I am so much interested in the general battle that I allow the banner of my division to be trailed in the dust . . . I am of no value to the Army."[9]

As a disciple of my Lord, in whom there was not a thread of spectatorism, I must take up arms in the battle for righteousness where God has placed me. I must be involved, and I must be focused. The advice of A. W. Tozer seems relevant and timely even today: "Pay no heed to the passing religious vogue. The masses are always wrong. In every generation the number of the righteous is small. Be sure you are among them."[10]

Elton Trueblood said, "It is perfectly clear that early Christians considered Christ their Commander-in-chief, that they were in a company of danger which involved great demands upon their lives, and that to be a Christian was to be engaged in Christ's service."[11]

But an observation Trueblood made of the mid-twentieth century church is perhaps even more true of the Church at the beginning of a new millennium. He said, "Perhaps the greatest single weakness of the contemporary Christian church is that millions of supposed members are not really involved at all, and what is worse, do not think it strange that they are not. . . . There is no real chance of victory in a campaign if ninety percent of the soldiers are untrained and uninvolved, but that is exactly where we stand now."[12]

As an enlistee in the Lord's army, I must be available, assignable, and dependable. I must fill my post through Spirit-filled soldiering. I must give account to my Commander-in-Chief. If I am faithful here, my faith will be contagious and the enkindling fire that Christ said He came to light (Lk. 12:49) will become incendiary. In the next chapter we shall look at some specific ways of making faith contagious.

# QUESTIONS FOR REFLECTION

1. Explain how Edith Schaeffer's statement about the family, "people throw away what they could have, by insisting on a perfection which they cannot have, and looking for it where they will never find it" applies also to the church?

2. Is it possible to have a church family that is free from all conflict? If not, why not?

3. What is most important in a church—people or programs?

4. How important are the "vows' that people make before a church altar? When uniting with a church?

5. What is all too often at the root of church conflict and disunity? But is this always true?

6. Discuss the concept of "abandonment" in relation to church conflict. Should it be an early option or a last resort?

7. What are the dangers of "spectatorism" in regard to developing personal and church growth?

# A PRAYER FOR SERIOUS FOLLOWERS

Dear Jesus, I realize that I am only one, and not "the only one" in the church. I know that there are many differing personalities, temperaments, and tastes in the body of believers.

I believe my church family to be the true "school of love." Teach me to listen and to love my brothers and sisters in Christ.

And, Jesus, teach me how to value my vows to You and to my church family. Let me be crucified to self and committed to the common goals and to the continuity of my spiritual family. In Jesus' name, Amen.

# CHAPTER NINE

# WILL I POSSESS A "JOHNNY APPLESEED" FAITH AND VISION?

*Jesus plan is to win the world by His followers—you and me, and He has no back-up plan.*

—Ron Sider

*Father, make me a crisis man. Bring those I contact to decision. Let me not be a milepost on a single road; make me a fork, that men must turn one way or another on facing Christ in me.*

—Jim Elliot

The first thing that Andrew did after personally responding to the call of Jesus, was to find his brother, Simon, and tell him, "We have found the Messiah" (Jn. 1:41, 2). Here is spiritual "spontaneous combustion." Here is the *message* (we have found the Messiah) and the *methodology* (he brought him to Jesus). This "combustion" is to work on both the personal level, and for the *church* (the collective body of believers).

Here is evangelism in its infancy: *having found*, and *telling others about my find*. Remember that Mark's gospel tells us that Jesus "appointed twelve—designating them apostles—that they might be with him and that he might send them out to preach" (Mk. 3:14).

This scripture is a "spiritual tintype." We must gather around Jesus regularly to worship Him and learn from Him, and then we fan out into the world, "showing and telling" others what we have absorbed from Him.

The word *preach* in Mark 3:14 does not mean that every follower of Jesus is to become an "ordained" minister or professional "clergy person." It *does* mean, however, that each follower of Jesus must become a full-time witness of Jesus' love and saving power.

## Propelled by a "Johnny Appleseed" Vision

My wife, Pat, lays claim to a genealogical link to that popular folk hero, John Chapman—better known as Johnny Appleseed. He was that colorful and unique American who planted tens of thousands of apples trees on the American frontier two centuries ago.

Johnny would gather apple seeds from cider mills, carefully plant them, then tenderly nurse the seedlings until he could resourcefully and creatively transport them to the settlers on the frontier.

Johnny not only planted orchards, but would often show up on a settler's doorstep, telling the family "What you need are apples." Spreading apple seed and seedlings became a passionate and propelling mission for Johnny.

Johnny was not only respected as a naturalist, nurseryman, and entrepreneur, but he was known and loved as a good man, by animals, Native Americans, and frontiersmen. And it is probably true that whenever he was temporarily staying with families, he would often pull out his old tattered Bible and read and tell stories to everyone's delight.

Imagine what would happen if Jesus' disciples would be as passionate about planting the seed of the gospel. I wonder what would happen in just my part of the world if I possessed a Johnny Appleseed faith and vision. It would surely propel me into fresh frontiers telling people—"What you need in your life is Jesus."

We even have an apple tree on our property that is an "off-spring" of the last living tree that Johnny Appleseed personally planted. It is genetically identical to the original "parent" tree. While we take some pride in that, we are far more excited about having spiritual offspring from the Jesus seeds we plant.

## Delivering God's Love Letters

God has written a love letter on the hearts and in the lives of His followers—a letter that He wants read by everyone they meet, wherever they go. James Lee West, in his moving article, "Get the Mail Out," explains that God has written a love letter, meant to be read by every person in the world. "It is really a proposal of marriage," says West, . . . "He wants to unite us with Himself. He is seeking to persuade humanity that He loves us so much that we in turn should fall in love with Him and be caught up in His purposes and in His life . . . God is mailing letters out all the time . . . to all the people of the world. . . . Each letter is stamped with the cross of Jesus Christ, and every letter is stained with His very own blood."[1]

Then, West likens the church to the post office, and he asks, "What's the purpose of the post office?" His answer is *to get the mail out*. We as Christ's followers, are God's love letters to the world. People are dying to read the mail from God through you and me, and the question every follower of Jesus must ask is: "Is the mail being delivered through me?" People most often read God's love letter to them first through another's life. Later they may read it in the Bible.

If I want to be like Jesus, I must have one overmastering passion—*to get the mail out*. That should be the controlling mission of my church also, and if it isn't it is my responsibility to prayerfully and tactfully remind them of the Master's Great Commission mandate.

It is neither wise nor biblical to feel that we must "shirt-collar" every person we meet, inquiring of their salvation, or insisting that they hear the "plan of salvation," or even for that matter, hear "our story." But, the born-again, Spirit-filled follower of Jesus will *be* a witness. That is the promise of Jesus.

## How to Make My Christianity Credible

One might well wonder and ask why it is that Christians are not making a greater impact upon the moral values in today's culture? Christian believers worldwide have always faced one huge problem—*how to make their Christianity visible and credible without becoming confrontational and intrusive.*

***I must incarnate Christ to my culture.*** God's grace must be actualized in life before it will be received by men. Our theology and doctrines must meet in human experience convincingly. Can this happen? Jesus answered this question by coming into the world. In Him, God's love and holiness became visible. "The Word became flesh and made His dwelling among us. We have seen His glory . . ." (Jn. 1:14a). Eugene Peterson's translation of John 1:14 comes to us with power and freshness: "The Word became flesh and blood and moved into the neighborhood."[2]

Having a "contagious" witness means that the Word must still become flesh. Now, the incarnation is in *you* and *me*, but the world must still behold *His* glory. Jesus' death and resurrection furnish the power for that to happen. We must furnish the receptacle for His life and love to fill. If I am a Spirit-filled follower of Jesus, I can relax, knowing that the Master has promised that I shall *be His witness, and that He will use my life.*

This does not mean that I shall never need to structure some intentionality into my witnessing or that I shall not need to learn how to better share my faith with others.

There is a wealth of information available on how to more effectively share the gospel and win our friends to Christ, and there are basic tools such as "The Four Spiritual Laws" (Campus Crusade for Christ), and "Life Can Have Meaning" (Beacon Hill Press), and "Peace With God," (Billy Graham Association), and numerous others. (See the simple plan for leading someone to Christ in the appendix.)

*Genuine love must characterize my life*. All techniques, strategies and plans for personal evangelism pale into impotence beside the dynamic of *love*. Love makes better sense out of the gospel than any doctrine or ethic that I might proclaim, and will validate any personal story that I might share with others.

This kind of love always has its origin in God and must center in Him. It has been said that sin is love's perversion. Sin makes self instead of God the object of its devotion and adoration. Sin is a sick, selfish, selective kind of love—love that has lost its true center.

True Christ-like love not only has its center in God, but has as its target all persons, even those who are difficult and unlovely. Francis Schaeffer writes: "All men bear the image of God. They have value, not because they are redeemed, but because they are God's creation in God's image. Modern man, who has rejected this, has no clue as to who he is, and because of this he can find no real value for himself or for other men. Hence, he downgrades the value of other men and produces the horrible thing we face today—a sick culture in which men treat men as inhuman, as machines."[3]

Love that reaches the unredeemed and the unlovely is not a soft, indulgent kind of love that is a cover-up for sin. It is a love that desires the holiness of others. Thus as Josh McDowell says:

"Tolerance says, 'You must approve of what I do.' Love responds,
'I must do something harder; I will love you, even
when your behavior offends me.'

"Tolerance says, 'You must agree with me.' Love responds,
'I must do something harder; I will tell you the truth, because I
am convinced the truth will set you free.'

"Tolerance says, 'You must allow me to have my way.'
Love responds, 'I must do something harder; I will plead with
You to follow the right way, because I believe you are worth
The risk.'

"Tolerance seeks to be inoffensive; love takes risks.
Tolerance glorifies division; love seeks unity. Tolerance costs
Nothing; love costs everything."[4]

Mildred Wynkoop wrote that for John Wesley, "holiness and love are one blazing unity of truth."[5] In other words, love without holiness is not love at all, and holiness without love is not holiness at all. Wynkoop also wrote that "holiness has to do with persons in relationship . . . and that has everything to do with life."[6]

Love is what Jesus was talking about in the Sermon on the Mount, and our world is wobbling badly because it has ignored the sturdy ethics of that great standard. If our faith is to become contagious, it will need a "blood" transfusion from that standard and my witness, both passive and active, must be saturated with divine love.

Love is the only dynamic for holy living and right relationships. Love breaks down walls and barriers. Love promotes *fellowship*. Sin destroys fellowship. Love produces harmony—but not the absence of creative conflict. Christian love must be tough enough to allow for strong differences of opinion without tearing apart the fabric of Christian unity.

*Forgiveness* is another characteristic of love that makes our Christianity credible and our witness contagious. Chuck Colson tells a story that beautifully illustrates the dynamic power of Christ's love. Two young men stood on a platform before a huge crowd of Catholics and Protestants. One of them, Liam, a Catholic, had been the last member of the famous Maze Prison hunger strikes, which took the lives of nearly a dozen IRA terrorists. Liam had starved himself for 55 days and was near death when his mother visited him and convinced him to break his fast.

While recovering, Liam gave his heart to Christ, and the love of God helped him to forgive those he once hated. Through his witness another man, named Jimmy, a Protestant terrorist, also came to know Christ. Now they stood side by side at the International Conference of Prison Fellowship Ministries in Belfast. In a powerful testimony, Liam put his arm around Jimmy's shoulders and said, "Before, If I had seen Jimmy on the street, I would have shot him. Now, he's my brother in Christ, I would die for him."[7] What a contagious witness.

***Love finds ways to help***. Love is not only *forgiving,* but it is also for *giving*. Love is ours to give away to persons who are in need. Love cannot remain *stored*. Love cannot be unconcerned and unmoved at the needs of others. Love cannot be exclusive or partial. My wife and I met him while spending a couple of nights at beautiful Glen Eyrie in Colorado Springs. He introduced himself as Jerry. He did plumbing and electrical work for the Navigator's Conference Center.

Jerry had with him a couple he was trying to help. He shared with us privately that the man had been in two or three prisons, and the woman had been a woman of the street. Yet Jerry had opened his own home to them. Risky? Perhaps, but love is vulnerable.

This bearded, warm, congenial layperson shared with me a deep concern he had. Very simply it was this. Christians talk love, but too often don't show it. Jerry and his wife had not only raised three children of their own, but had taken in many others through the years.

Later, a staff person with Navigators said to me. "Jerry always has someone with him that he is helping." Not everyone will have the gift of helping "down and outers" like Jerry does, perhaps, but all of us have the gift of God's love to share with others. His story simply demonstrates how concrete our love must become if it is to be credible to a skeptical world. The greatest thing I can do for God is making His love visible.

John R. W. Stott says, "Although every Christian is not called to be a minister or a missionary, God does intend every Christian to be a witness to Jesus Christ. In his own home, among his friends in his college or at his place of business, it is his solemn responsibility to live a consistent, loving, humble, honest, Christlike life, and to seek to win other people for Him . . . the way to begin is by prayer. Ask God to give you a special concern for one or two of your friends . . . pray regularly and definitely for their conversion . . . foster your friendship with them for its own sake; take trouble to spend time with them; and really love them for themselves."[8]

*Love begins in the home or family*. There is one place, more than any other where it is absolutely crucial that a loving witness happen—in my own family. There is no crisis in the culture today as great as that facing the family or the home. Kenneth Chafin says, "We need to become aware that the future of the country is being settled not by ambassadors, congressmen or presidents— but by parents."[9]

Dr. James Dobson of Focus on the Family, warned two decades ago that "the institutions of marriage and parenthood were not the invention of mere men and women; they were designed and sanctioned by God Almighty. He created the family and the principles which make it work. If we deviate from His plan to substitute our own puny schemes, we will witness the disintegration of everything of value and meaning."[10]

Edith Schaeffer in her classic, *What is a Family*, says a family is "an ecologically balanced environment for the growth of human beings."[11] Her succinct definition is a reminder of the sacred purpose of the family for growing and maintaining people who are healthy emotionally, psychologically, and spiritually. Our families turn out people who either grow up to love or to hate, bless or curse—people who will either be a part of the world's problems, or a catalyst in the solution of those problems.

While there are many deviations from God's ideally balanced family environment, such as one-parent families or "blended" families, we need to be reminded of God's norm, and the ideal, when we are in danger today of losing sight of it. We need also to be reminded that God always works with whatever is available to Him, regardless of how fragmented the family might be or for whatever reason. It is all the more important then that God's love and grace be demonstrated.

## Is There a Church in the House?

The church, in the truest sense, is the body of believers, wherever they might be individually—in the temple, on the job, in the marketplace, or in the home. But the church *in the home* has more power for shaping character and culture than any other unit of influence, or all the others combined.

The challenge, then, must be to get the church back into the home. That is the ultimate arena for our witness and missionary service. The "church" in the home is a family of persons who love God and each other so much that there is a commitment to each other for life. Godly living in the home will produce godly living in the street and in the halls of government. Private righteousness will spawn public righteousness.

The question "Is there a family in the house?" is an important and relevant one for today's culture, but an even more important question is, "Is there a church in this house?" or "Is the family in this house a church?" For unless the family is Christian, there's not much hope for its survival or for intergenerational continuity of faith and values.

In the first century, the church literally gathered in individual homes as is indicated by 1 Cor. 16:19 and Col. 4:15, which refer to "the church that is in their house." The museum at Yale University contains a room, 9 x 22 feet, which was brought all the way from Iraq. The room is identified as the kitchen of a house once occupied by a devout Christian family of the third century.

Scholars theorize that this private house was a gathering place for worship and fellowship by Christians. The most fascinating fact about this room is that after more than fifteen centuries the whole world can see that it belonged to those who loved Jesus Christ and served Him.

Perhaps the aim of every Christian believer should be to help create that kind of climate and leave that kind of imprint upon their own families and homes. My first witnessing and missionary assignment is to "go home to my own family and tell them what great things God has done for me" (Mk. 5:19).

## But What About My Witness in the Public Square?

It is not likely that too many questions will be raised about my exercising a strong Christian witness in my own home or in my church. My right and privilege for expressing my faith in the "public square" is quite another thing. Opposition is sure to surface here.

One might expect voices in the secular world to be promoting the "privatization" principle—the notion that strongly held religious and moral views should be expressed only in personal and private spheres, never in the public debates or domain. What may be surprising and a bit confusing to many, however, is that there are voices coming today even from within the religious community itself counseling the same. Some religious leaders are calling for "unilateral disarmament" by religious activists, demanding that they use different weapons and strategies to impact the culture.

The focus of Christians in the culture wars, according to these pacifist strategists, should be almost exclusively upon "living holy lives," and proclaiming a "higher and better" kingdom.

***Should disciples become social activists?*** So just what are Christian disciples supposed to do? How active can or should we be in seeking to confront or change our culture—to influence and change government policy and societal conditions?

John Whitehead says, "We (in America) are witnessing the end of traditional religion (especially Christianity) in the public sphere . . . America is moving toward *religious apartheid*."[12] But can Christians quietly and Biblically live with apartheid?

John Wesley wrote: "making an open stand against all ungodliness and unrighteousness, which overspreads our land as a flood, is one of noblest ways of confessing Christ in the face of His enemies."[13]

Who has not been inspired by the story of Dietrich Bonhoeffer and the "Confessing Church" during the Nazi reign of terror? And who would suggest that William Wilberforce should have remained silent in the face of the infamous slave market in nineteenth-century Britain? Or that Dr. Martin Luther King should have remained in the safety of his church instead of carrying the battle for civil rights into the streets and the public square?

One can only imagine what conditions might be like today, had there been more such activists. Francis Schaeffer wrote: "most fundamentally, our culture, society, government, and law are in the condition they are in, *not because of a conspiracy, but because the church has forsaken its duty to be the salt of the culture.*"[14]

Did not Jesus say, "You are the salt of the earth. But if the salt has lost its saltiness, how can it be made salty again? It is no longer good for anything except to be thrown out and trampled by men" (Mt. 5:13).

Glen Tinder in *The Political Meaning of Christianity*, says, "Christians should be a sobering presence in the political world," adding that "the notion that we can be related to God and not to the world . . . is in conflict with the Christian understanding of God."[15] Madeline L. 'Engle put it so simply: "It is impossible to listen to the Gospel week after week and turn my back on the social issues confronting me today."[16]

Thus many Christians believe Christianity and spirituality must touch every sphere of life, and that religious isolationism is out of sync with the Bible and will only serve to accelerate moral decline in any society.

***What are the risks in social activism?*** Christian disciples should not expect that entering the public square and confronting their culture is without peril either to their specific cause, or to the cause of Christ in general. Whitehead cautions: "Christians should approach the political process not as crusaders seeking to vanquish the infidels, but as servants anxious to share the benefits of Christian values."[17]

Christians who get involved in politics must be careful that their cause not become the "mistress" of some political ideology. They must constantly remind themselves that the kingdom of God will not be ushered in through politics, presidents, or kings, but only by the King of Kings. Only God can save the world.

Even in countries where free elections are allowed—perhaps especially in such, hope can be misplaced. Again, Whitehead cautions that "Christians who rest their faith in the next election are practicing a form of idolatry."[18]

Commonsense wisdom laced with love even for those with whom Christians disagree is essential. It is easy to oversimplify issues, and to reduce every issue to a clash of good and evil. "Christians must be aware of their own fallibility. Humility, not extremism, should characterize Christians."[19]

Christians will not gain much of a hearing if they boldly rage against abortion and homosexuality, yet ignore racial and gender discrimination, conditions of the poor, and reckless disregard for the environment.

Perhaps the greatest risk adheres to *institutional* activism. Robert Dugan wisely suggests: "Our Christian politics will be more effective and less objectionable if we emphasize individual involvement rather than institutional involvement."[20] For a church to marry itself to a particular candidate or party is not only foolish, but illegal. It is to risk losing the tax-exempt status. Even worse, would be the risk of losing a soul God has brought under the church's care.

*As Christ's disciples we must be "salt" and "light" in our culture.* Nevertheless, pastors can and should address *moral* issues from their pulpits, and as private citizens, are constitutionally guaranteed freedom of expression and involvement. And it is disturbing to imagine what our culture in America would be like without the savor of organizations like Focus on the Family and the American Family Association.

Christians have their feet planted in two cities—the City of God and the City of Man. They cannot escape either. And surely it is inescapably clear that Christians cannot leave the City of Man without light from the City of God. We must, however, be tolerant in our views about how to best "light up" that city.

Robert Dugan says, "Under any form of government, a Christian's first political assignment is intelligent intercession for politicians."[21] The Apostle Paul wrote, "I urge, then, first of all, that requests, prayers, intercessions and thanksgiving be made for everyone—for kings and all those in authority, that we may live peaceful and quiet lives in all godliness and holiness" (1 Tim. 2:1, 2). One wonders how different our world might be if Christians faithfully practiced this one exhortation alone.

What additional involvement is expected or desired may always be open to some debate. It is likely that some Christians are better equipped by temperament, by education, and by experience to effectively engage the culture publicly.

Those skeptical of social and political activism on the part of Christians point to the Christian believers in China, observing that though persecuted and driven underground, the church has flourished—not seeking to change the policies of a Communist government, but simply by faithfully practicing their faith.

The splendor of holy lives in the midst of the sordid ugliness of an evil culture is undoubtedly the best hope for the redemption of that culture, and is what the gospel is all about. Still, it is difficult to imagine God being pleased with any form of religious apartheid that would be indifferent to a political and cultural slide into tyranny and societal decadence.

A Jewish rabbi, Daniel Lapin, says of America, "We really have no choice but to pray and encourage a return to an America steeped in Judeo-Christian values. It is either that or taking our chances in a society with no values at all. For all Americans the former carries certain risks, but the latter spells certain doom."[22]

Charles Colson reminds us: "While the battle rages on planet earth, we can take heart—not in the fleeting fortunes of men or nations, but rather in the promise so beautifully captured in Handel's *Messiah*. Stop. Listen. Over the din of the conflict . . . you will hear . . . 'The kingdom of this world has become the kingdom of our Lord and of His Christ.'"[23] No longer Caesar and God, but God alone. But until then, we have our feet in two cities.

I must then give attention to the credibility of my witness for Christ. What kind of "wallpaper" do I display on the monitor of my "life-screen"? Whether in the privacy of my home or in the public square, if my faith is not viewed as authentic and attractive, it certainly won't be contagious.

But, will I have to be able to answer all of the questions raised by those I'm trying to reach? In the next chapter we shall examine this issue.

## QUESTIONS FOR REFLECTION

1.  Does the thought of personally witnessing for Jesus create fear and panic, or excitement and adventure?

2. Have I carefully evaluated what Jesus said in Acts 1:8 about witnessing?

3. What are the distinctive meanings of the words, *evangelist, preach, witness,* and *minister?*

4. What is it more than anything else that will make my life and testimony a *credible* witness?

5. Is it necessary to learn how to share a "plan of salvation" in a formal or "canned" sort of way?

6. Am I willing to share a simple "before and after" story of the change Jesus made in my life? Are there ways I could improve my story or the sharing of that story?

7. How private or public must I be with my faith? Is "religious apartheid" an option for today's Christian?

---

## A PRAYER FOR SERIOUS FOLLOWERS

Father, never let me forget that I am intended to be a "love letter" from You to all the persons whose lives I touch. Don't let me fail to "get the mail out."

May I be ever alert as to how I can better incarnate your love. Give me the courage to be the salt and light needed not only in my private home but also in the public sphere.

Help me to simply tell *my story*—how You changed my life and gave me a reason to live and a reason to die. Above all, give me the passion for souls that characterized Your Son who said He had come to *seek and to save* the lost. In His name, Amen.

# CHAPTER TEN

# MUST I HAVE ALL THE ANSWERS?

*The problem of reconciling human suffering with the existence of a God who loves, is only insoluble so long as we attach a trivial meaning to the word love.*

> —C. S. Lewis

*But for the night, "the moon and the stars, which thou hast ordained," would never be seen. And so God giveth to His own "the treasures of darkness."*

> —Oswald Chambers

*None of us believers will be purified except in the fire of inward pain.*
> —Michael Molinos

Scott Peck's bestseller book, *The Road Less Traveled,* begins with a less than comforting statement: "Life is difficult." Indeed it is, and it is often very difficult for the Christian as well.

Jesus never promised any of His followers a path free from pain, suffering, heartache, or even life's hassles. He said, "In this world you will have trouble. But, take heart, I have overcome the world"

(Jn. 16:33). He also warned, "If they persecuted me they will persecute you also" (Jn. 15:20). George MacDonald said, "The Son of God suffered unto death not that men might not suffer, but that their sufferings might be like His."[1]

And to the would-be follower, who almost boastfully said to Jesus, "Teacher, I will follow you wherever you go," Jesus replied, "Foxes have holes and birds of the air have nests, but the Son of Man has no place to lay his head" (Mt. 8:19,20).

Jesus never promised that discipleship would be easy. In fact the heart of His invitation included the necessity of *taking up one's cross*. "If anyone would come after me, he must deny himself and take up his cross and follow me" (Mt. 16:24).

Dietrich Bonhoeffer said, "The cross is not the terrible end to an otherwise god-fearing and happy life, but it meets us at the beginning of our communion with Christ. When Christ calls a man, he bids him come and die."[2]

Michael Molinos, the seventeenth century Catholic mystic, the possession of whose writings meant ex-communication from the church, said, "I would assure you that after you have given yourself up to the Lord—to walk with Him and live in Him, *in an inward way*, all hell will conspire against you."[3]

Oswald Chambers wrote: "Watch what the Bible has to say about suffering, and you will find the great characteristic of the life of a child of God is the power to suffer, and through that suffering the natural is transformed into the spiritual . . . happiness is not a sign that we are right with God; happiness is a sign of satisfaction. That is all, and the majority of us can be satisfied on too low a level. Jesus Christ disturbs every kind of satisfaction that is less than delight in God."[4]

C. S. Lewis wrote that "It is for people whom we care nothing about that we demand happiness on any terms: with our friends, our lovers, our children, we are exacting and would rather see them suffer than be happy in contemptible and estranging modes.

. . . God has paid us the intolerable compliment of loving us in the deepest, most tragic, most inexorable sense."[5]

The disciple's spiritual journey will include plenty of pain, pests, and other tests. And it will surely include a large bundle of *whys—questions* that one must answer for him or herself—and questions that the world expects the Christian disciple to have an answer for, rightly or not.

We're talking questions like: Why does God allow bad things to happen to good people? Did God create evil? If God is all good and all powerful why doesn't He just put an end to evil and suffering immediately? Didn't God say, "Ask, and it shall be given"? Why, then, does God not heal everyone who asks for it?

## What Do I Do with This Bundle of Why's?

Some Christians, especially new converts and disciples, sometimes fear that they will not have answers for the critics, skeptics or scoffers, or even for their own questions or doubts. They also fear that they will not know how to discern truth from error—whether they are hearing the voice of God, their own environmentally-shaped ideas or the distorted and inaccurate ideas of others—or maybe even the voice of the arch-deceiver, Satan.

It is important for me, a follower of Christ, to know that if I have been born of God's Spirit and filled with God's Spirit, I can take comfort in knowing that Jesus promised that He would guide me into all truth. Jesus said, "But the Counselor, the Holy Spirit whom the Father will send in my name, will teach you all things, and will remind you of everything I have said to you" (Jn. 14:26). I can relax in that assurance, but I need not feel that I must have an *immediate and instant* answer to all of life's mysteries.

*How then, can I discover answers that are true?* Jesus said, "Whoever follows me will never walk in darkness, but will have the light of life" (Jn. 8:12). There are at least four things that can help guide me as a disciple into that light: 1) a knowledge and understanding of God's written Word, 2) staying close to Jesus through worship and prayer, 3) loving obedience to the "light" I already possess, (if anyone chooses to do God's will, he shall find out . . . Jn. 7:17) 4) the godly counsel of trusted spiritual mentors or counselors (including a regimen of Christian reading such as suggested in the appendix.)

No, I will not need to become a theologian, but God has gifted each of us with minds to inform and discipline, and with a free will. Lazy or complacent Christians neither discover answers nor make good disciples.

Not knowing all the answers about the Bible, God, life, the origins of the universe or life, sickness, pain and death, need not cause me embarrassment or diminish my faith in God. Indeed, there will be times when I must humbly confess "I am not sure I can answer that question at the moment, but I am willing to seek the truth, and I am confident that God will help us to discover the truth.

Even the Bible, which contains more "answer ore" than we can ever mine, declares that "now we see but a poor reflection as in a mirror; then we shall see face to face. Now I know in part; then I shall know fully, even as I am fully known" (1 Cor. 13:12).

Dennis Covington has written, "mystery is not the absence of meaning, but the presence of more meaning than we can comprehend."[6] Be patient. Many answers will come with diligent inquiry and maturity, but we will never have all the answers. To demand that life be denuded of all mystery is a futile and self-destructive path.

*We must trust God anyhow.* Philip Yancey has written quite perceptively in regard to faith when faith is challenged by adversity. He says, "I have concluded that faith requires obedience without full knowledge. Like Job, like Abraham, I accept that much lies beyond my finite grasp, and yet I choose to trust God anyhow, humbly accepting my position as a creature whose worth and very life depend upon God's mercy."[7] And Chambers says, "The very nature of faith is that it must be tried; faith untried is only ideally real, not actually real."[8]

J. Henrich Arnold writes simply: "learn to trust Jesus always, even when you cannot understand something. Situations often arise in life without your understanding why. The only answer is to trust Jesus."[9]

In the world's view of things, "*Seeing* is believing," but the true disciple has a different "modus operandus"—"*believing* is seeing." Again, Yancey writes, "we receive enlightenment only in proportion as we give ourselves more and more completely to God by humble submission and love. We do not first see, then act: we act, then see . . . and that is why the man who waits to see clearly before he will believe, never starts on the journey."[10]

The disciple of Jesus can be "knocked out of shape" by temptation, evil, suffering, and death, or even by the overwhelming mysteries of life. There are answers to many of life's questions for those who are willing to *search* for them, or *wait* for them as may be required. Obviously this is not a book that can tackle all of the theological, philosophical or practical questions regarding the difficulties one can encounter in following Jesus. For that one would need the world's great libraries.

We would touch upon only three issues that seem to be especially troubling to saints and sinners alike—and they are issues that seem to "dog" the disciple's steps from day to day, if not generation to generation—the problem of suffering and healing, the problem of origins, and the question that Pilate asked before Jesus, "What is truth?"

These three are chosen as representative of the kinds of questions and mysteries that Christian disciples must deal with, but need not be overwhelmed by. Necessarily, the scope of this book disallows depth treatment of even these issues. Additional sources will be found in the appendix.

## How Should We View Suffering and the Question of Healing?

Obviously there are all kinds of suffering and by no means is it limited to the physical, but since the questions regarding physical suffering and the possibilities of healing are so immediate and so persistent, our focus will be there.

**Fact one:** *Suffering is universal. Jesus' followers are not exempt.* Jesus asserted that His Father causes the sun to rise on the evil and the good, and sends rain on the righteous and the unrighteous (Mt. 5:45).

**Fact two:** *Healing was a vital part of Jesus' ministry when He was here on earth.* Matthew said, "Jesus went throughout Galilee teaching in their synagogues, preaching the good news of the kingdom, *and healing every disease and sickness among the people* (Mt. 4:23, emphasis mine). And to the leper who came to Jesus, saying, "Lord if you are willing, you can make me clean," Jesus simply said, "I am willing . . . be clean," and "immediately he was cured of his leprosy" (Mt. 8:2,3).

**Fact three:** *Jesus gave to the "twelve" and to the "seventy" disciples authority not only to preach, but also to heal* (Mt. 10:1,8; Lk. 10:19). They were active in this ministry even after our Lord's ascension and in the Early Church. Although some Bible scholars view these phenomena (healing and other miraculous interventions) as primarily dispensational, Christian literature and testimony would indicate that many miraculous healings and signs are still taking place today.

**Fact Four:** *We have the privilege of asking for healing.* There are many things that we don't receive as Christians simply because we do not ask. And, according to the Bible, there are some things we ask for and do not receive because we ask with the *wrong motive*. But Jesus told His followers to "Ask," that they might receive.

One does not need to neglect the blessings of modern medical science to enjoy the advantages of praying for healing. God expects His children to make full use of the fruit of medical research and knowledge and training. God is still the miracle of all medicine and the Lord of all healing

Perhaps some are negligent in praying for divine healing for fear of being considered "radical," or afraid of what people will say if they are *not* healed. The fact that some have abused the privilege of praying for healing by commercializing it, or treating it like a "fetish" does not in the least diminish its power or value. What good and legitimate thing has not been abused?

**Fact five:** *God often answers prayer for healing, directly and supernaturally intervening.* There is a tablet in the back of a church in Lucknow, India which reads: "near this spot Stanley Jones knelt a physically broken man and arose a physically well man."[11] E. Stanley Jones, by his own testimony was a man at his "ropes end" in his early missionary work, but he went on from his healing in 1917 to give fifty-four more years of fruitful evangelism to the world. He called it an "unconditional" healing—direct, radical, and instantaneous.

This is just one of countless thousands of well-documented modern examples of divine healing. *Guidepost* and other magazines are filled with first-person case histories of God's intervention and healing.

**Fact six:** *God never withholds His mercy, but for reasons that are not always clear, He does not always heal in the way we want Him to.* David Ford writes, "It is clear that prayer is not magic or a slot machine. God is not a God of quick fixes and easy instantaneous solutions. Signs of hope are given but God is above all concerned with love, and long-term faithfulness, with healing hearts, minds, and communities as well as bodies."[12]

God is more interested in our holiness than in our physical healing. This is a distinction that is hard to keep clear in a "fallen world" with its preoccupation with the material and with immediate comforts. The connection no doubt explains some of the delays and denial in answer to prayer.

C. S. Lewis called pain "God's intolerable compliment." God's very mercy and love for me may prevent His dashing to my every discomfort with instant deliverance. He desires my total wholeness and healing—spiritually as well as physically.

Shelden Vanauken's beautiful love story, *A Severe Mercy*, is an account of how God had to break through the "shining barrier" of his and his wife's tightly insulated love. Shelden was led to see, through the letters of his friend, C. S. Lewis, how his wife's death was simply a "severe mercy" from God intended to bring him into a relationship with God that his love for his wife, Davy, had excluded.

Glaphre, who has had a powerful impact upon our times with her prayer ministry, said of her own efforts to cope with disease, "I was wanting God to change my circumstances. God was wanting to change me."[13] God allows some sickness and suffering in this world in order to effect a more perfect and permanent healing for eternity.

## Keeping Holiness and Healing in Balance

The connection between holiness and healing will protect us from an unbalanced Scriptural view of healing. A balanced perspective on the whole of Scripture as well as human experience must not only acknowledge the possibility of great cure by praying for healing, but also the possibility of continued suffering and of succumbing to physical disease even when the sincere prayer of faith is offered.

E. Stanley Jones was unconditionally healed early in his life and ministry as previously mentioned, but much later he suffered a stroke from which he was not healed. Yet out of this "handicap" he was to write his final and beautiful book, *The Divine Yes*. The book describes God's keeping grace *in the midst of sickness*.

While the atonement has achieved full provision for healing and deliverance, God will remain sovereign. He will not be manipulated even within the triumphs of the atonement. Neither will He be confined to our time scheme. Again, Glaphre writes pointedly about this: "A dangerous exchange this—this switching roles with God. This belief that God must act on *our* conclusions of what is best and needed. This requiring God to fulfill *our* desires *our* way." She continues: "What happens when God doesn't jump through the hoop we hold up? Especially when the hoop-jumping and errand hopping is the only kind of help we want from God."[14]

Calvin Miller points out that God does not exist to make us happy. He says, "anyone who holds such a preposterous view is going to have a miserable relationship with God. He does not lavish his children with a jolly discipleship so that they may swim in spiritual ecstasy between conversion and death. God is a giver, but He does not give happiness. He gives redemption, meaning, security, love, victory, and the indwelling of the Holy Spirit."[15]

As David Ford writes: "Because our suffering is so intolerable we are also tempted to try magical, quick-fix solutions that do not do justice to the depth of the problems."[16]

And what if there are no simple and final answers to the question of suffering and healing in this life? Can I stand this, my soul? Who after all, can understand how God could or would suffer for all mankind on that dreadful but glorious cross?

The important thing is that we must not be intimidated by some popular "priest" of the health-wealth-and-prosperity cult who claims to "understand it all," and tells you that if you aren't healed you simply do not have enough faith, or there is sin in your life. A simple reading of the great "faith" chapter, Hebrews 11, will quickly cure that misinterpretation of Scripture.

Admittedly there are some promises that people are not appropriating, but equally there are some premises being promoted that just don't square with the whole of Scripture or with human experience. While there are without doubt many miraculous cures, one cannot establish an unfailing precedent upon these. God is too great, humanity is too deep, and individualism too significant for God's methods of dealing with men and their diseases to become stereotyped.

Geoffrey King believes that God allows some suffering in the world to gender sincere and true sympathy. He says, "If we could cure every sickness, the heart of this world would become as hard as stone."[17] And Ford writes: "suffering is the greatest teacher; the consecrated suffering of one soul teaches another."[18]

Further, he writes, "through the prism of my tears I have seen a suffering God," but he quotes Nicholas Walsterstoff who "rethinks why it might be that we cannot see the face of God and live: The sorrow in that face would be too much for us."[19] Oh how He suffered that we might find the wholeness and holiness that we need.

Mother Teresa, that godly helper of humanity, who has seen so much of the world's suffering, says, "suffering, pain, humiliation, feelings of loneliness, are nothing but the kiss of Jesus, a sign that you have come so close that He can kiss you."[20]

Certainly what I have written here will not answer many of the questions about evil and suffering in the world or in the life of a disciple, but if we had all the answers we would need neither God, nor faith. Philip Yancey writes: "my own life of faith has included many surprises that no one warned me about. Of course, if the journey did not include a few potholes, dark stretches, and unexpected detours, we would hardly need faith."[21]

James writes to encourage and inform the first-century believers, "Consider it pure joy, my brothers, whenever you face trials of many kinds, because you know that the testing of your faith develops perseverance," and he adds, "blessed is the man who perseveres under trial, because when he has stood the test, he will receive the crown of life that God has promised to those who love him" (Jas. 1:2, 3, and 12).

## What About the Question of "Origins"?

Of all the questions that the Christian disciple must grapple with, none is more important than the question regarding "origins." Where did I come from? How did I and the world around me get here?   Because this question is so persistent, fundamental, and crucial to the Christian worldview, the author includes it in this chapter on finding answers.

God has spoken very clearly in His word regarding the source of life. "In the beginning God created the heavens and the earth" (Gen. 1:1). And John, in the beautiful prologue to his gospel, wrote: "In the beginning was the Word, and the Word was with God and the Word was God. He was with God in the beginning. Through Him all things were made; without him nothing was made that has been made. In him was life and that life was the light of men" (Jn. 1:1–4), and the Apostle Paul, writing to the early believers at Colosse, and speaking of Christ, said, "He is the image of the invisible God, the firstborn over all creation. For by him all things were created: things in heaven and on earth, visible and invisible, whether thrones or powers or rulers or authorities; all things were created by him and for him. He is before all things, and in him all things hold together" (Col. 1:15–17). *We must then, either trust God's Word or end up questioning the authority of the Holy Scriptures.*

Now modern science has also spoken regarding this issue. The dominant view within the scientific community regarding first causes or origins for the universe and life is simply that of the philosophy of *naturalism*. Naturalism claims that God did not create us. We created God for our own delusional comfort.

Naturalism denies any existence transcending the material world and believes that all that *is* is the product of random, unsupervised forces in nature. All life generated from a single cell born in a primordial soup of chemicals.

As Charles Colson puts it: "Naturalism begins with the fundamental assumption that the forces of nature alone are adequate to explain everything that exists. Whereas the Bible says 'In the beginning God created the heavens and the earth' (Gen. 1:1). Naturalists say that in the beginning were the particles along with blind, purposeless natural laws. That nature created the universe out of nothing through a quantum fluctuation. That nature formed our planet with its unique ability to support life. That nature drew together the chemicals that formed the first living cell and naturalism says that nature acted through Darwinian mechanisms to evolve complex life-forms and, finally, human beings with the marvels of consciousness and intelligence."[22]

Yet there are many scientists who do not subscribe to the hypothetical conclusions of the larger body of the scientific community. Today, many scientists are concluding that "evolution" is not even good science.

Unfortunately for science and for all who are sincerely in search of truth, early on in the twentieth century, science had an "unholy marriage" with naturalistic philosophy. Philip Johnson, a Berkeley law professor, author, and lecturer, put it this way: "The authority of science was captured by an ideology, and the evolutionary scientists thereafter believed what they wanted to believe rather than what the fossil data, the genetic data, the embryological data and the molecular data were showing them."[23]

Obviously, good science wants to see detectable empirical evidence that God is interactive with the world. Enter then what today is known as the "intelligent design" movement—scientists who believe that it is not possible to explain the irreducibly complex and information-rich structures of biology without acknowledging an intelligent first-cause.[24]

Stephen Meyer, a Cambridge-educated PHD, believes that "design" now constitutes the best explanation for the origin of the "information" required to make a living cell in the first place.[25] For example: The information storage density of DNA is several trillion times that of our computer chips. Organisms display any number of features of intelligently engineered high-tech systems: transfer capability, functioning codes, sorting and delivery systems, feedback loops, independent networks. "For this reason," says Meyer, "the biology of the 'Information-age' now requires a new science of design."[26]

Although evolution has been a "tightly closed system" of thought, today there are many reputable, credentialed, and highly honored scientists who are daring to attack the "king on the mountain."

The author of this book is not a scientist and does not wish this chapter to be an attack upon science as such. There are many great scientists who are sincerely seeking the truth wherever that truth may lead. And one shudders to think where society would be without our scientific research in so many different areas of knowledge.

Scientific research, unencumbered by the presuppositions of "naturalism" is no threat to God's truth and will in fact, this author believes, ultimately confirm God's Word. Francis Bacon once said, "a little science estranges a man from God. A lot of science brings him back."[27]

As Colson says, "when it comes to the origin of life science is squarely on the side of creation by an intelligent agent. We have nothing to fear from the progress of science."[28] The "Intelligent Design" movement does not say that God is the "Intelligence" or the "Designer," but it doesn't need to.

As a disciple of Christ, I will not need to have all the answers regarding the apparent age of the earth, the fossil records, or the Big Bang theories to keep a simple trust in Jesus as the Lord of creation and the Lord of life. The Psalmist said, "the earth is the Lord's, and the fullness thereof, the world and they that dwell therein" (Ps. 24:1, KJV), and the inspired writer of Hebrews says, "For every house is built by someone, but God is the builder of everything (Heb. 3:4). It's all His and we are never wrong to be openly seeking the truth. Jesus said, "Then you will know the truth and the truth will set you free" (Jn. 8:32).

But *truth* leads us to the final question that the twenty-first century disciple must grapple with—*what is truth?*

## Are There Any Absolute Truths?

As a Christian disciple journeying through the twenty-first century, I will obviously encounter many of the familiar road hazards that have threatened disciples in every century: pride, temptation, materialism, discouragement, resentment, complacency, and the like. But there are some perils peculiar to the new century that one needs to be aware of.

The heart of modernism in the nineteenth and twentieth centuries was the search for truth through "human reason" alone. The disciplines of science and education were to be the "divine deliverers" from our social disorder and dysfunction. Transcendent truth was discounted or ignored.

Gene Veith says, "Modernists did not believe the Bible is true. Postmodernists have cast out the category of truth altogether."[29] Truth to the twenty-first century postmodernist is never *objective* or *propositional.* It is what is called a "social construct." It is in fact whatever a particular person or group of persons want it to be to accomplish their particular goals.

If Christians make any sense at all out of the postmodern culture, they will have to view it through this lens: *the abandonment of truth and absolutes.* Truth for society in this ultra-relevant culture will increasingly be determined by the public's circling of a number on a ten-point scale rather than by the Ten Commandments of God.

Clearly this has multiple risks. *Pluralism* rushes in to fill that vacuum. Pluralism itself may be innocent enough—meaning only "more than one"—the existence of many kinds, persons, groups, ideas, or options. But pluralism in the hands of many will bring sinister designs and changes.

Truth and life's values can be smothered by too many choices and options. Os Guinness writes, "Life is now a smorgasbord with an endless array of options. Whether a hobby, vacation, lifestyle, worldview, or religion, there's something for everybody—and every taste, age, sex, class, and interest. The church of your choice? A liturgy to your liking?"[30]

The criteria for choosing one's church or religious beliefs can be no deeper than that of choosing which fast food restaurant to visit. Gene Veith explains, "Aesthetic criteria replace rational criteria . . . 'I really like that church,' they will say . . . religion is not seen as a set of beliefs about what is real and what is not. Rather, religion is seen as a preference, a choice. We believe what we like."[31]

Without an objective standard of truth and surfeited with too many options, the possibility for syncretism and diluted Christianity looms large. Furthermore the likelihood of deep religious commitments diminishes. Guinness says, "pluralization acts like a spiritual Teflon, sealing Christian truth with a slippery surface to which commitment will not adhere. The result is a general increase in shallowness, transience, and heresy."[32]

Pluralism also touches humanity at its deepest level—*relationships*. It puts "a unique strain on Christian marriage, which as it disintegrates puts an added strain on the plausibility of faith and the stability of the church."[33] Vows and commitments are not so meaningful, for there are always other options—other spouses, other churches, other friends and other employers.

The morality of postmodernism has been called the "morality of desire." What I want and what I choose is right and true for me, and who are you to question my desires and my choices? Of course this is only rank existentialism and the old immorality, but postmodernism gives it new attire and "respectability" with the abandonment of truth and absolutes.

One of the cardinal virtues of postmodernism is *tolerance*. At its worst, pluralism sees all ideas, all religions, and all cultures of equal worth. Christians will be shamed for thinking or claiming to have "the only truth," and will be labeled "narrow" and "judgmental." The only sin may very well be to call anything *sin*.

As a disciple I am, first of all, a learner of Jesus. I know that there is truth, for Jesus declared, "I am the way, the truth, and the life" (Jn. 14:6). Jesus said, "you shall know the truth, and the truth shall set you free."

I must be aware of the trends of our times. The deconstruction of truth is in full swing. But, as Gene Veith writes: "Truth exists, though it often eludes us, and we may fail to grasp it perfectly . . . what God reveals in His Word is absolutely true. These truths can be reasoned upon, fit together with other truths, and applied."[34] Veith recalls what Francis Schaeffer has pointed out: "what the Bible reveals is true, but it is not exhaustive. The Bible does not reveal *every* truth about God or the world."[35] It does reveal all we need to know about God's love for us and the way of salvation.

When "Christian" and "Faithful" were passing through Vanity Fair, they were asked what they would buy, and their answer was: "We buy the truth" (Prov. 23:23). Bunyan wrote that "at that there was an occasion taken to despise the men the more; some mocking; some taunting; some speaking reproachfully; and some calling upon others to smite them."[36] One of the citizens of Vanity Fair said of Christian and Faithful that "they were enemies to, and disturbers of, their trade; that they had made commotion and divisions in the town, and had won a party to their own most dangerous opinions . . ."[37] Let all who would pursue truth know that from the Fall of mankind in the Garden, the world has never wanted to "buy the truth." The truth always threatens unrighteous living.

Furthermore, twenty-first century disciples must carefully distinguish between "information" and *truth*. Does the "information highway" necessarily lead us to more meaning or truth? Douglas

Groothuis quotes the French philosopher, Jean Baudrillard, who says, "we live in a world where there is more and more information and less and less meaning." Groothuis also quotes Neil Postman here: "The tie between information and human purpose has been severed, i.e., information appears indiscriminately, directed at no one in particular, in enormous volume and at high speeds, *and disconnected from theory, meaning, or purpose.*"[38]

While postmodernism brings perils, it also brings promise and exciting possibilities. Surrounded by cheap imitations, the *diamond of truth* will sparkle more brightly, and the desire for genuine holiness will quicken. The church must cherish and preserve the truth, but proclaim it charitably, not defensively—a flaw of fundamentalism in the twentieth century.

As our global society becomes increasingly multi-cultural, the mission field comes to our own doorstep. Opportunities for cross-cultural evangelism explode. The first-century A.D. was similarly marked by pluralism, and yet the church powerfully impacted that culture. It will be done again.

Our destination as twenty-first century disciples is no different from Christian pilgrims in previous centuries. The postmodern highway will cut through a different cultural terrain, with some new perils. Prepare to be annoyed. Truth will be up for sale, but God's children have the truth in Jesus and in His written Word.

Os Guinness wrote: "Like an eternal jack-in-the-box, Christian truth will always spring back . . . no power on earth can finally keep it down. Out of a mid-eastern grave rose the Son. As Saint Augustine put it, 'The cross of the Lord became the devil's mousetrap.'"[39]

As disciples, we will not be able to decipher all of life's mysteries, but filled with the Holy Spirit and equipped with the Word of God, we can know all that we need to know to make our Christian pilgrimage through this life. And, hopefully, it can be said of us as it was of "Gibbie" in George MacDonald's *Sir Gibbie*, "he would run to do the thing he had learned yesterday, when as yet he could find no answer to the question of today."[40]

But does that mean I will never fail God or fall? The next chapter addresses the subject of what a disciple should do when he or she has failed the Lord.

## QUESTIONS FOR REFLECTION

1. What, in your view, are some of the most urgent and important questions that people deal with in regard to the Christian faith and life?

2. Which of these are the most relevant, or perhaps even troublesome to you personally?

3. What do you think C. S. Lewis meant by calling human pain "God's intolerable compliment"?

4. Can we expect, as Christians, to have answers to all of our questions and life's mysteries?

5. What advantage does a Christian disciple have over the nonbeliever or unconverted in dealing with suffering and life's mysteries?

6. What relationship exists between healing and holiness in God's economy of grace?

7. How significant is the question of "origins" in one's worldview?

8. Explain the concept of the emerging scientific movement called "intelligent design"?

9. What are the dangers of "pluralism" in regard to truth?

## A PRAYER FOR SERIOUS FOLLOWERS

Father, we know that you have endowed us with intelligence and inquiring minds, and that you welcome our questions, but you have many ways of keeping us reminded of our finiteness.

When your Word is straightforward with answers, I will believe it, and when I don't understand or find answers I will humbly trust you. I know that you have chosen to work within the parameters of our self-sovereignty, and you desire our love and holiness more than our physical wholeness or happiness.

Above all, Father, I will keep my focus upon your Son, Jesus, who plainly said, "I am the *way*, *the truth*, and the *life*." My faith is fixed on Him. In His name, Amen.

# CHAPTER ELEVEN

# WHAT SHALL I DO WHEN I'VE FAILED GOD?

*Come now, let us reason together, says the Lord, though your sins are like scarlet, they shall be white as snow; though they are red as crimson, they shall be like wool.*

—Isaiah 1:18

*When God forgives, He never casts up at us the mean, miserable things we have done. "I have blotted out, as a thick cloud, thy transgressions, and, as a cloud, thy sins." A cloud cannot be seen when it is gone.*

—Oswald Chambers

*No temptation is more terrible than to be without temptation.*

—Dietrich Bonhoeffer

No one wants to fail, but there are none who *never* fail. That is true even for those seeking to follow Jesus in serious discipleship. The Apostle James says simply: "We all stumble in many ways" (Jas. 3:2). We should not *plan* to fail or *expect* to fail. Nor should we view sin as inevitable, but the reality is that there are none who haven't failed God in some manner.

Regarding spiritual failure, Hannah Whitall Smith writes: "There ought not to be (failures), and need not be; but as a fact there sometimes are, and we must deal with facts, and not theories . . . there are very few, if any, who do not confess that, as to their own actual experience, they have at times been overcome by at least a momentary temptation."[1]

Norval Hadley writes, "The angels and Adam came right from the Maker's hands 'with no proclivity toward disobedience, yet there was that possibility of sinning which is implied in free agency,' . . . if all possibility of sinning were removed for the sanctified Christian, he would be placed above Adam and Eve. He would be a moral machine."[2]

The grace of God does not cancel our humanity. We will always have this treasure of God's grace in what Paul called "earthen vessels" (2 Cor. 4:7). W. T. Purkiser has put it this way: "We have a sinful self to be crucified with Christ, a human self to be controlled by Christ, in order that the true self may be realized in Christ."[3]

It is never impossible for a human soul to fall into sin or spiritual failure regardless of one's state of grace or growth and maturity. Nevertheless, the inspired writer, the beloved John, says, "My dear children, I write this to you so that you will not sin. But if anybody does sin, we have one who speaks to the Father in our defense—Jesus Christ, the Righteous One" (1 Jn. 2:1).

The tense and thought of the Greek here is "that you not sin even once." So here we find no allowances for the inevitability of sin—or the excusing of sin as a practice. But our concern here is what should happen if we find that we have failed God or sinned against our blessed Savior.

## What "Not" to Do in Time of Failure

The important thing is to know what to do when one discovers that he or she has been tripped up by a "surprise sin," or for that matter, has failed God for any reason under any circumstance. Let us look first at what *not* to do.

The testimony of the great saints through the ages as well as the testimony of the Word of God is quite unanimous. First, do not panic or despair or utterly cast away your confidence. Our spiritual enemy, Satan, would like nothing better than to get you to believe that you have committed the "unpardonable" sin for the slightest of offenses, and to convince you that there is no use for *you* to try to live for God. Maybe someone else, but *you* are hopeless.

Then sets in that most lethal of weapons that Satan uses—*discouragement*. If he can get the "fallen disciple" enveloped in a gloom of discouragement, he knows, in that weakened condition the disciple is much more vulnerable to even further failure and, ultimately, total defeat.

## What *Should* I Do When I've Failed God?

What shall I do, then, when I've failed God? There's a good computer word for this. It is *reboot*. Sometimes as computer operators we find that our system crashes. When it does, it can be very frustrating, and we may be tempted to do as the fellow in the television commercial—push it out the window.

But, it is important in such times not to panic. It may be distressing or even humiliating, but often the problem is not that difficult to fix. It requires patience and determination to stick with the job. In our spiritual lives, when our operating system crashes—when there is spiritual failure of any kind, God wants us to "reboot" our system and not throw away our faith or our work.

In dealing with spiritual failure, as Hannah Whitall Smith writes: "From whatever cause we have been betrayed into failure, it is very certain that there is no remedy to be found in discouragement."[4] The great point of recovery is to be found in an *instant return to God*.

Smith writes, "the same moment which brings the consciousness of sin ought to bring also the confession and consciousness of forgiveness. This is especially essential to an unwavering walk in the life hid with Christ in God, for no separation from Him can be tolerated here for an instant."[5]

Naturally our spiritual enemy will discourage this immediate return to God. Indeed, our own minds will recoil against this instant reconciliation, but for a different reason. As Smith asserts, "our feeling is that it is presumption, even almost impertinent, to go at once to the Lord, after having sinned against Him. It seems as if we ought to suffer the consequences of our sin first for a little while, and endure the accusings of our conscience; and we can hardly believe that the Lord *can* be willing at once to receive us back into loving fellowship with Himself."[6]

But this is a "false humility" that is designed to trap us. The enemy of our souls knows that the longer we delay our return to conscious, sweet fellowship, the more likely we are to continue on the path of alienation and destruction. The more instant the return, the less likely a recurrence of the same or a similar sin. And what if there is a recurrence?

*I must keep getting up:* Shall the one who told His disciples to forgive seventy times seven, be less merciful than He expected his disciples to be? Certainly, we should make no license for a "sinning religion." Sin is not to be trifled with, nor is the mercy and grace of God to be treated lightly. God's Word and God's grace were made possible at enormous cost—the Cross, and they make possible not only forgiveness for sin, but *deliverance from sin*. God says, "Be holy for I am holy" (1 Pet. 1:16). God does not require what He cannot enable.

But the "good news" of this chapter is that if one slips and falls in his or her walk with God, like a child who stumbles and falls while learning to walk, yet looks up through tears and finds the smile and encouragement of the parent, so the fallen disciple must get up and learn to walk. Jesus is merciful. He will grant grace and power to the disciple learning to walk with Him.

The Bible says, "Let the wicked forsake his way and the evil man his thoughts. Let him turn to the Lord, and he will have mercy on him and to our God, for he will freely pardon" (Isa. 55:7). Also, "If we confess our sins, He is faithful and just and will forgive our sins and purify us from all unrighteousness" (1 Jn. 1:9). Many saints in the past have had to pray the words of Psalm 51 on their knees not once or twice, but many times. If you have failed God, turn to that psalm right now.

A simpler prayer of confession is what is called "The Jesus Prayer" which says, "Lord Jesus Christ, Son of God, have mercy on me." This prayer has been used by multitudes and when uttered in sincerity is at once a confession of the Lordship of Christ and His identity with our humanity, and a simple plea for His mercy.

Paul wrote "But now He has reconciled you by Christ's physical body through death to present you holy in His sight, without blemish, and free from accusation if you continue in your faith, established and firm, not moved from the hope held out in the gospel" (Col. 1:22, 23a).

We must guard against sin, but if we do sin, we have a merciful Father who is more interested in getting us to heaven than we are to get there ourselves. God, who forgave us initially when we were first saved or born again, doesn't suddenly become a "tyrant" just waiting to punish us or strike us down at the first sign of weakness and failure. "For God did not send His Son into the world to condemn the world, but to save the world through Him" (Jn. 3:17).

Consider what your attitude would be when your own child has done wrong, yet comes to you in true sorrow and repentance. Shall we expect less from our Heavenly Father?

## It is Better to "Prevent" Spiritual Failures Than to Repair Them

"Not again," I protested to myself, pumping the accelerator pedal, but finding no power.

"This dumb car is going to kill me yet," I said out loud this time, as I engaged the clutch and hit the starter.

Fortunately, the motor started and I cleared one of the busiest intersections in town without getting clobbered. I spent the remaining time driving home, wondering why this modern, sophisticated machine called an automobile was failing me. I needed performance and dependability, and I thought I was paying for both.

Pulling into our driveway, I swung the car door open, when it suddenly occurred to me to check the service sticker on the door post. A quick glance back to the odometer startled me. "Surely not! Nine thousand miles? That can't be," I thought. But it wasn't lying.

As I headed toward the front door of my house, my embarrassment now slowed my pace measurably. I knew this car might be performing badly because "someone" was neglecting simple car-care procedures. I didn't need a mirror to discover who that someone was.

Now mind you, my car-care "intentions" were very good. I had a desire to keep this car in top-notch condition. I had just been so busy. I was preoccupied with other interests. There was no plan— no reminders.

One of the leading car manufacturers has a maintenance plan called SMART. It stands for "scheduled maintenance at regular times." They advertise that "protection is smart for one of your larger investments—your vehicle." This car manufacturer insists that regularly scheduled maintenance keeps minor problems from becoming major and expensive ones. Makes sense for Christian living too.

And now, I was asking myself, "Do I have a larger investment than my spiritual life vehicle?" Wouldn't it be smart to have a plan for my spiritual life, too? A kind of soul-care plan to *prevent* failures rather than having to *repair* them. C. Neil Strait comments that "someone gave good advice when he said, 'prepare and prevent rather than repair and repent.'"[7]

It might be a simple apology that needs to be made before it leads to a major "carbon collection" of resentment. Neglect of Bible reading, prayer, or church attendance can clog up my spiritual "fuel injectors." A failure to confess some sin may lead to a spiritual "foul out."

SMART discipleship will seem expensive and an intrusion at the time, but it will actually avoid enormous cost and inconvenience down the road in my journey with Christ.

My car may not need *daily* care, but my soul will. My relationship with God is on a "sovereign" basis. It is "personal" and involves choices made out of love—not feelings or rigid mechanics.

Like the marital relationship, it cannot be ignored for a single day without suffering. "Planned togetherness" is essential in keeping alive any sovereign relationship, whether with my spouse, my children, or my God. Togetherness doesn't just happen in this busy modern society.

Admittedly, the idea of a daily "quiet time" does not excite the average action-oriented Westerner. If it comes early in the day, the lure of all those "important" assignments and chores clamors for my attention. If it comes at the close of my day, it is too much like an "Amen" to all the "real" work of the day. And how sleepy I can get saying that "Amen"!

Another enemy of SMART discipleship is the *time trap*. We are victims of a culture that has never had more time-saving devices and *less* time. There is only one cure for this malady. We must simplify our lives and refuse much of this "glittering and clamoring clutter."

Conditioned by a culture of comfort and ease, studied discipleship has little appeal to the masses. In his book, *The Taste of Joy,*

Calvin Miller says, "Never has there been so many disciples who did so little studying," and he cautions that "no lazy student ever felt good on report-card day."[8]

Recalling Miriam's beautiful song of deliverance in Exodus 15, Miller comments that, "Moses was less of a spiritual cheerleader than his sister Miriam. It is not recorded that he played the tambourine, but he did write down the books of the law . . . they used these laws for the next 3,000 years."[9]

Inspiration is great, but tambourines can be fickle and moody. We need to build our lives on something substantial. SMART discipleship will put into practice the recommendations of chapter six in this book, and keep a careful monitor of one's relationship with God.

A CPU without a "monitor" would not be very useful. We need a "window" that displays and monitors the processes and the progress of our projects. In our spiritual lives, God has planned that prayer, Bible study, and regular worship habits, and servanthood should provide insight and checks and balances into our spiritual well-being.

SMART discipleship is not a novel idea, only a neglected one. Desire, creativity, and resourcefulness can liven up one's daily quiet time, but the battle will probably be won in the trench of tough-minded discipline. There must be a stern rebuke to the flesh which says, "I will have a carefully guarded time of togetherness with my Lord. Nothing shall steal that from me."

That is SMART discipleship. It will protect me. It will prevent major spiritual breakdowns. It will give me "high-octane" performance for my daily journey with Christ. But if I have failure, I will remember to make an instant return to God, trusting in His mercy and His grace, and keep on walking with God.

Will there be temptations? Absolutely. Even our Lord was not exempt from them. The familiar temptations of pride, self-will, and sinful pleasures will be used by Satan in every generation. But, are there some temptations that will be peculiar to the new century and millennium? No doubt many that we are yet to identify, and some that are beginning to emerge.

For example, despite the exciting promise and potential of our high-tech culture, Douglas Groothuis says that the god of technology may lack "official shrines, altars, tax-exempt organizations, and clergy. But it is a god, nevertheless."[10] Not everyone would agree with Groothuis perhaps, but he warns that "cyberspace may be the greatest temptation yet offered to humanity to lose its soul in diversion."[11]

Still, I will remember with Paul Rees that "the preoccupation of the New Testament epistles is not with sin, or defeat, or frustration in the Christian life . . . their preoccupation is with Christ— Christ our righteousness, Christ our power and our adequacy, Christ for cleansing and for conquest!"[12]

The writer of Hebrews says, "do not throw away your confidence, it will be richly rewarded . . . let us throw off everything that hinders and the sin that so easily entangles, and let us run with perseverance the race marked out for us. Let us fix our eyes on Jesus, the author and perfecter of our faith . . ." (Heb. 10:35, 12:1, 2).

I need to stay in the race for my own reward and good, but there is another reason I must be faithful and overcome. God wants to use my life in a special and unique way. In the next chapter we will explore His magnificent plan for His disciples.

## QUESTIONS FOR REFLECTION

1.  Is sin "inevitable" in the life of a disciple of our Lord?

2.  In society, if one is accused of breaking the law and remanded to court, one of the first things he or she will need

and is assured of is an attorney. Who will be the advocate of the Christian believer who has sinned or failed God?

3. What is the one thing a Christian should *not* do in the event of any kind of spiritual failure?

4. What is the greatest point of recovery in the case of sin or spiritual breakdown?

5. What is one of the best Psalms to read on our knees if we have failed Christ?

6. Explain the difference between "repair jobs," and "preventative maintenance" in one's spiritual journey?

7. What is SMART discipleship? Does it have a place in my Christian life?

## A PRAYER FOR SERIOUS FOLLOWERS

Dear Jesus, I long to be perfectly pure in heart, righteous in living, and fervently loyal to You, and I pray for the courage and discipline to apply preventative maintenance to my life.

Please, Jesus, deliver me from all spiritual pride, for your Word warns that "pride comes before a fall." Should I sin or fail you for any cause, and even for a moment, let my heart quickly fly back to your heart, and let my feet stay in the race.

Thank you for your mercy, dear Lord. Like the waves of the ocean, the tides of your mercy keep pounding the shore of my life. I am reminded that "God did not send His Son into the world to condemn the world, but that the world might be saved through Him." In Jesus' name, Amen.

# CHAPTER TWELVE

# DO I KNOW HOW GOD WANTS TO USE MY LIFE?

*It is the privilege of every Christian to have a sense of destiny about the person that he is and the things he aspires to do for Christ. He can know that the very grain of the universe somehow runs in the direction of his best and noblest desires and that all of reality will work to bring to pass the bright design of God for his life.*

—Dave Breese

*I knew that no king, no president, and no ambassador had a more exciting assignment than I had in just bearing witness to Jesus—the Way, the Truth, and the Life.*

—Stan Meek

As a disciple, I will, of course, know that God wants to reveal his own life, power, and glory through my life. God surely wants to "showcase" His grace in a beautiful and most meaningful way in each individual believer.

What could be a greater purpose for living than simply to "bear witness" to Jesus by a holy lifestyle—by words, by actions and reactions, and by my attitudes and dispositions? When Jesus was on trial before Pilate, He said, "for this reason I was born, and for this I came into the world, *to testify to the truth*" (Jn. 18:37, emphasis mine).

## A Powerful Purpose for My Life

One day early in my ministry I read those words of Jesus and pondered them carefully. I realized that for myself at least, I had just discovered a powerful new, but simple purpose for my life. I reasoned this way: If Jesus, God's Son, could say, "For this reason I came into the world—to bear witness to the truth," then surely I could have no greater reason or purpose for my own personal existence.

From that time, I began each day with a thrilling thought throbbing in my heart and mind—*today, I have the privilege of "showcasing" Jesus*—of mirroring His love, His life, His Spirit. Whatever else I think I must get done, or whatever else is on my agenda, I realize that it is of lesser importance than the goal of just being a good witness for Jesus—"the Way, the Truth, and the Life." *And I know that no king, no president, and no ambassador ever had a more exciting assignment.*

So again we are reminded of the words of C. S. Lewis that "God works on us in all sorts of ways. But above all, He works on us through each other. Men are mirrors, or 'carriers' of Christ to other men."[1]

But while this is undoubtedly the ultimate and bottom-line assignment that God has for every one of his disciples, I believe that God has something else special and unique in mind for each individual believer. No two snowflakes or oak leaves are exactly alike. Your fingerprint and DNA are distinctive, and God doesn't just have a one-size-fits-all plan for His disciples. You are unique. I am unique. No one else in the world has my exact personality, temperament, flow of experiences or life history.

## Becoming a Difference-maker

A disciple must not only be different from the world, but a disciple must be a "difference-maker." Do I know how God wants to use me to make a difference in my world? Unfortunately too few of Christ's followers know precisely how God wants to use them.

Ken Blanchard asks a couple of key questions: "Do you really know yourself? Do you have a personal 'mission statement' that defines your strengths and motivates you to be all God meant you to be." Blanchard says, "If you have trouble with that question, you might want to try an interesting activity that will almost certainly help you develop a clearer purpose and personal identity: Write your own obituary." Blanchard continues: "I know it sounds strange—even a little morbid. But this exercise is not about dying, it's about living. It will give you an opportunity to adjust your life, describe the ideal you, and define what it is you would like to be remembered for. Why leave such important matters to chance? God has a wonderful plan for your life. Let Him help you establish your path and guide you as you walk in it."[2]

George Barna says that as Christians, "we hunger to invest our time on earth in activities that have spiritual significance. Such meaning comes by understanding how He created us and how we can employ every resource at our disposal—time, energy, money, relationships, materials, knowledge—to unfold God's ultimate plan for humankind."[3]

As the twenty-first century and a new millennium break upon us, the outlook for something spiritually significant happening may seem dim. Since September 11, the threat and reality of world terrorism has left a pall hanging over the whole world. As George Barna writes: "objectively speaking the future offers little hope. Violence, pornography, broken families, substance abuse, poverty, life-curtailing diseases, natural disasters, international wars, illiteracy, racial animosity, appear on the list of hardships and cultural deterioration. Yet vision-directed Christians maintain the most optimistic and hopeful perspectives about the future. They are, after all, *involved in the spiritual redemption and interpersonal redevelopment of the world*, employed by the Lord Jesus Christ."[4]

Somewhere I read this statement: "Because of Jesus, hope got up before the sun." It is true, of course. As a disciple of Jesus I should be one of the world's first-class hope spreaders. The sun is not setting. It is just peaking over the eastern horizon for God's kingdom builders in the twenty-first century. God placed me here. Do I know how He wants to use my life?

## But Does God Have a "Unique" Plan for My Life?

While this is a book of discipleship for "ordinary" Christians in the new millennium, that does not mean that God doesn't have a unique plan for my life nor that He may not tap you or me for being a great leader or "catalyst" disciple. God has always chosen ordinary people to carry out extraordinary assignments.

Barna says, "The Father of all creation has prepared you for such a time as this. It is an exciting and opportune moment in the course of human history . . . God is counting on you to rise to the occasion. He has designed and gifted you in a particular way, allowed you to have certain experiences, and has provided you with opportunities that will contribute to the fulfillment of His heart's desires for His creation."[5]

## Discovering My Special Gifts

God has endowed each one of us with natural gifts and abilities, and with certain "spiritual gifts." We need to know ourselves and to discover what our spiritual gifts and individual aptitudes and temperaments are, and ask God to help us use these for His glory.

The Bible mentions at least 27 spiritual gifts:

| | |
|---|---|
| Administration | Knowledge |
| Apostle | Leadership |
| Celibacy | Martyrdom |
| Deliverance | Mercy |
| Discerning of Spirits | Miracles |
| Evangelism | Missionary |
| Exhortation | Pastor |
| Faith | Poverty (voluntary) |
| Giving | Prophecy |
| Healing | Service |
| Helps | Teaching |
| Hospitality | Tongues (languages) |
| Intercession | Wisdom |
| Interpretation | |

Most of the above gifts can be found in these five passages of Scripture: Romans 12:6–8; 1 Corinthians 12:8–10 and 28–30; Ephesians 4:11, and 1 Peter 4:9–11. As a follower of Christ, I can be certain that I have at least one of the above gifts, and most likely several of them. The purpose of God's spiritual gifts is to do God's will and work for the benefit of others.

Barna reminds us that "spiritual gifts are meant to form a complementary matrix within the Body of Christ, to be used in a seamless web of interlocking efforts that build the church."[6]

There are excellent temperament tests and spiritual gifts analysis inventories available. Two such would be: "The Trenton Spiritual Gifts Analysis" by Fuller Evangelistic Association, and "The Keirsey Temperament Sorter" found in the book *Please Understand Me: Character and Temperament Types* by David Keirsey and Marilyn Bates.

As a follower of Jesus I am in the Lord's army. The total army has a mission. Each division, company and platoon has a mission, but platoons are made up of individual soldiers, each with specific assignments. The success of the army is dependent upon individual soldiers that are well-trained, and highly disciplined. But being disciplined does not exclude intelligent, creative, and visionary thinking. God has created each of us in His own image.

An important difference, however, is noted between being in a national army and being in the Lord's army. In God's army, at each juncture, each step of the way, I have a choice. My Commander-in-Chief will never press me into service against my own will. Nor will He insist upon my serving in roles for which I have no gifts, abilities, or interests.

Again, Barna writes: "You are serving in His [God's] army to change the course of human history. You have the privilege of exerting influence in unfolding world events, and you have the honor of playing a role in unfurling God's great plan for His creation."[7] But Barna believes that "fewer than one out of twenty believers has discovered God's vision for his or her life and ministry."[8]

## What Is Vision?

At this point, we might well ask, "What is Vision?" According to Barna, "vision is a clear and precise mental portrait of a preferable future."[9] It is seeing in advance the difference God wants to make with my life, in my family, in my church, in my community, and in the world. Barna explains, "Vision is not a solution to a current problem. . . . Vision is not a quick fix. It is a long-term solution to long-term opportunities."[10]

For example think of the difference the Apostle Paul's life made. Paul didn't just believe that his conversion to Christ should result in a changed personal life, and leave it at that. He knew he should become a "difference maker." Paul had a vision for evangelizing the Gentiles and nurturing their faith by organizing new churches throughout the Roman empire. As Barna says, "Paul was the quintessential visionary believer. The only love I know that compels bravery and foolishness such as he exhibited is the love of Christ."[11]

Contemporary examples of vision-driven Christians might be Martin Luther King and James Dobson. King's dream was to strip segregation of its moral legitimacy, create a color-blind society, and restore the sense of dignity and self-respect that blacks had lost. Dobson, on the other hand, "convinced that the family is the basic building block of society and that when the biblical prescription for family development is tampered with, disastrous results are inevitable, engineered an extensive web of services (Focus on the Family), designed to encourage the church and families and to protect the family from harmful cultural and governmental attacks."[12]

The author is not suggesting that each disciple with a vision will have such an enormous impact upon the culture. We will not all be Kings, or Dobsons, much less Apostle Pauls, but "having a vision" can allow a disciple to focus his or her life in a laser-like fashion and make a greater difference.

Dwight Moody once said, "Give me a man who says, 'this one thing I do,' and not 'these fifty things I dabble in.'" True disciples of Jesus have a profound sense of destiny about their lives. "The authentic follower of Christ is committed to growing in an honest and profound relationship with God. One important outgrowth of that pursuit is our desire to be a more serious and reliable servant of the king."[13]

## Find Out What God Is Up to and Get in on It

I must get in on what God is up to in this world. In seeking to discover my gifts and to understand myself better, I must realize that all of this can become too self-centered. When I begin to follow Jesus, I am no longer the center of my universe—Jesus is. I should first find out what God is doing in this world and ask Him how He wants to employ me in His unfolding plan for the world—and for my own backyard.

Chambers says, "When God gives a vision and darkness follows, wait; God will bring you into accordance with the vision He has given if you will wait His time. We try to do away with the supernatural in God's undertakings."[14]

Take heart, dear friend, God is more interested in getting you into the right niche than you are. He will guide you through His Word, through prayer, and through a bit of effort on your part to understand your temperament, your spiritual gifts, and your own experience.

Henry Blackaby says, "When God purposes to do something through you, the assignment will have God-sized dimensions. This is because God wants to reveal Himself to you and to those around you. If you can do the work in your own strength, people will not come to know God. However, if God works through you to do only what He can do, you and those around you will come to know Him."[15]

Again, Chambers reminds us, "If we try to do God's will through our own effort we produce Ishmael. Much of our modern Christian enterprise is 'Ishmael,' ie., it is born not of God, but of an inordinate desire to do God's will in our own way—the one thing Our Lord never did."[16]

Above all, remember that God's greatest assignment for you is simply to model Him before a love-starved world. Mother Teresa said, "We must know that we have been created for greater things, not just to be a number in the world, not just to go for diplomas and degrees, this work and that work. We have been created in order to love and to be loved."[17]

She has challenged us all by her selfless example and by these words "give yourself fully to Jesus. He will use you to accomplish great things on the condition that you believe much more in His love than your weakness."[18]

What are the icons on my spiritual "desktop"? I should ask God to help me arrange the desktop of my life so that my mission, goals, activities and priorities best fulfill His destiny for my life.

Dave Breese writes, "It is the privilege of every Christian to have a sense of destiny about the person that he is and the things he aspires to do for Christ. He can know that the very grain of the universe somehow runs in the direction of his best and noblest desires and that all of reality will work to bring to pass the bright design of God for his life."[19]

On the other hand, we must always keep in mind what Oswald Chambers reminds us of, "Our Lord's conception of discipleship is not that we work for God, but that God works through us; He uses us as He likes, He allots our work where He chooses, and we learn obedience as our Master did (Heb. 5:8)."[20]

Chambers also says, "It is God who engineers circumstances. Abraham refused to see this, and every now and again he stepped in and engineered circumstances for himself, and every time he did this, he upset everything."[21]

The true disciple does not try to engineer the circumstances of his or her life, but simply knows and loves the Engineer, and is willing to trust Him with the journey.

In the next chapter we shall look at what makes that journey successful.

## QUESTIONS FOR REFLECTION

1. What is at least one simple, single-defined purpose that any disciple should have for his or her life?

2. Besides being a mirror of Christ's love and image in the world, in what other unique ways might God want to use my life for His glory?

3. How could writing my own "obituary" help me to develop a "mission statement" for my life?

4. Have I ever taken a spiritual gifts inventory or a temperament sorter to assist in discovering my personal strengths, gifts, and personality traits?

5. How would I define "vision" in relation to my life?

6. Explain what you think Oswald Chambers meant when he said "much of our modern Christian enterprise is "Ishmael"?

# A PRAYER FOR SERIOUS FOLLOWERS

Lord, my greatest goal in life is simply to bear witness to You—your magnificent love and grace. I hunger to invest my time on this earth in ways that have deep spiritual significance.

Help me, dear Jesus, to discover the unique design that you have for my individual life so that I can not only be different from the world, but a "difference-maker" wherever I am.

Above all, may I be spiritually sensitive to what You are up to in the world and get in on it. In Jesus' name, Amen.

# CHAPTER THIRTEEN

# WHEN IS DISCIPLESHIP SUCCESSFUL?

*The test of the life of a saint is not success, but faithfulness as a steward of the mysteries of God in human life as it actually is. (Lk. 6:41)*
—Oswald Chambers

*Show business belongs to the pagan order of things; devotion to God in actual human conditions belongs to the Redemptive order.*
—Oswald Chambers

What, after all, is successful discipleship? What is pleasing to God? Are there some criteria by which we can measure ourselves? Oswald Chambers wrote that one of the biggest snares for the Christian is "the idea that God is sure to lead us to success."[1]

Elton Trueblood writes: "It is clear that Christ never allowed any of His followers to suppose that participation in His cause, if it were genuine would be easy . . . Christianity gives much to its adherents, but *it is always perverted when it is presented as a success story* . . . it is, instead, a relationship which begins with a dangerous and uncalculating commitment."[2]

There is a very real danger in this postmodern, "success-intoxicated" society of evaluating our discipleship by the standards of a high-tech, consumer and market-driven culture. Wealth, production, performance, profits, competency, results, and even health, are the big concepts.

## Spiritual Fruit Is Rooted in a Relationship

Certainly God expects our lives to be a witness, to make a difference, and to bear fruit for Him. Jesus did say, "This is to my Father's glory, that you bear much fruit, showing yourselves to be my disciples" (Jn. 15:8). Obviously these words inform us of the importance of making our lives count for God, but we must put them in context, and the context reveals just what Trueblood insightfully suggests—that discipleship is rooted in a relationship—a relationship with Jesus Christ. *That relationship forms the core of successful discipleship.* That relationship is of greater worth to God than ever our performance could be.

Has there ever been a more beautiful metaphor of spiritual life and that relationship than that painted for us by the Master Gardener in John 15? Jesus pictures Himself as the "true vine," His disciples as the "branches," and His Father as the Heavenly Gardener (v. 1). And, He insists that just as in nature a branch has to remain in the vine if it is to produce foliage and fruit, so the disciple must "remain" in a healthy relationship with the Vine (Himself).

Jesus says, "I am the Vine; you are the branches. If a man remains in me and I in Him, he will bear much fruit; apart from me you can do nothing" (v. 5). Jesus was using repetition here for He had already declared in verse 4 that *no branch could bear fruit by itself.* It must remain in the Vine.

## Staying Connected Is the Essential Goal

And that repetition is seen even more graphically in the word *remain*. Jesus uses that word *eleven* times in the first ten verses of this chapter. And in the context of the vine and the branches, *remain* can only mean "stay connected." The Contemporary English Version puts it this way: "Stay joined to me, and I will stay joined to you. Just as a branch cannot produce fruit unless it stays joined to the Vine, you cannot produce fruit unless you stay joined to me. I am the Vine, and you are the branches. *If you stay joined to me, and I stay joined to you, then you will produce lots of fruit.* But you cannot do anything without Me. If you don't stay joined to me, you will be thrown away. You will be like dry branches that are gathered up and burned in a fire" (Jn. 15:4–6, CEV, emphasis mine).

So, how can I (a branch) stay connected or joined to Christ (the Vine), so that I may bear fruit that will glorify God (my Heavenly Gardener) ? Jesus is quite explicit in providing answers to that question. He says, "As the Father has loved me, so have I loved you. Now remain in my love. *If you obey my commands* you will remain in my love just as I have obeyed my Father's commands and remain in his love. I have told you this so that my joy may be in you, and that your joy may be complete. My command is this: Love each other as I have loved you. Greater love has no one than this that he lay down his life for his friends. You are my friends if you do what I command" (Jn. 15:9–14a, emphasis mine).

Chambers writes, "The spirit of obedience gives more joy to God than anything else on earth . . . the best measure of a spiritual life is not its ecstasies, but its obedience."[3]

It's pretty easy to see that the way to stay connected to Jesus is through *love* and *obedience*. We're talking *sacrificial* love here, for Jesus insists that we love each other *as He loved us*. A love that is willing to lay down one's life for his friend. Jesus says we can stay connected to His love, if we will be obedient to Him even as He was to His Heavenly Father.

> As mentioned earlier, somewhere along the path that I have followed in my discipleship journey, a powerful statement of truth impacted my life. The statement: "When I am prepared to be to Jesus all that Jesus was to His Father, Jesus will be to me all that His Father was to Him." I have lost track of the source of that truth, but I immediately inscribed it into the front of my Bible, and have meditated upon that truth and tried to live by it.

It appears that Jesus had a secret by which He lived His life in the flesh—His life in this world. That secret furnished the dynamic for His accomplishing what He did—living and ministering in the power of the Spirit and accomplishing not less than our own salvation on the cross. And the beautiful thing about Jesus' secret, He doesn't keep it a secret *from anyone who really wants to know the truth.*

## Jesus' Relationship with His Father

We discover that secret as we observe Jesus' relationship with His Father. So what was His relationship to His Father? Well, first, *Jesus had a hidden life with His Father.* He was always looking at His Father's face, always *watching* what His Father was doing, and always *listening* to His Father. We readily detect this as we study His life. He had a hidden life of communication with His Father. One cannot fail to observe the times of prayer that Jesus, the Son of God, immersed Himself in. If Jesus felt the need of prayer, and made time for it, surely the rest of us should understand our need of that vital and direct communication with God.

Secondly, *Jesus was committed to do His Father's will.* The sole purpose of Jesus was bound up in the purpose of God. "Our Lord's life is the exhibition of the will of God, not of doing the will of God," says Chambers.[4] Jesus had no plans apart from God's, and

He was never distracted from that. Over and over, Jesus said things like, "I must do the will of my Father." Jesus sensed that He was in this world on a divine mission. A disciple of Jesus must know why he or she is here, and once realizing that, must never be distracted from that mission.

Jesus was committed to the Father, identified with the Father, and available to the Father. Jesus did what He saw the Father doing and said what He heard the Father saying. He said, "I tell you the truth, the Son can do nothing by himself; he can do only what he sees his Father doing, because whatever the Father does the Son also does. The Father loves the Son and shows him all he does" (Jn. 5:19, 20a).

Note: Most of us have too many plans of our own to really be watching and listening to what the Father is saying and doing and wanting to do in this world. Those who will be the most effective in their discipleship will be those who have no *personal* agenda, only a *Christ-agenda*. **When I am prepared to be to Jesus all that Jesus was to His Father, Jesus will be to me all that His Father was to Him.**

No wonder then he told His disciples: "I tell you the truth, anyone who has faith in me will do what I have been doing. He will do even greater things than these because I am going to the Father. And I will do whatever you ask in my name, so that the Son may bring glory to the Father. You may ask me for anything in my name, and I will do it" (Jn. 14:12–14).

## Keep the Son in Your Eyes

It may seem strange, but perhaps nothing could illustrate the essence of successful discipleship better than a pet we once owned named Kristi.

When I married my wife, Pat, I thought sure I was going to hear the words, "Will you take this woman, her paint horse, and her shadow dog to be your lawfully wedded companions?" For this reason, plus, I confess my own affinity for animals, we have had a dog or two for most of our fifty plus years of marriage.

Each one of them has loved and been loved and added an extra dimension to our lives. The popularity of James Herriot's books attest to not only his skill as a storyteller, but of the powerful emotions people have toward their animals. Herriot also has reminded us that the "Lord God made them all." If the Lord made them, who would doubt that they can teach us valuable lessons?

Perhaps Kristi taught us the most about devotion and discipleship. When we acquired Kristi, we had to drive two hundred miles south to pick up a cute four-month old German shepherd puppy. Although Kristi was none too excited to be going with her new owners, the long trip home lying on the floorboard of the car at Pat's feet helped to determine the direction of her devotion forever.

The scent of her new master combined with petting and feeding from her hand fixed her loyalty. Isn't it something like that with the Lord. Once we have drunk in the scent of the Rose of Sharon, and have received His provisions of love and grace, can we ever have a different Master?

Close observation of the *relationship* between Kristi and her master across the years reveals a few secrets that could help any disciple. First, *Kristi keeps her master in sight.* She lies where she can always see her. If her master changes locations in the room, she relocates also. If her master leaves the room, Kristi follows. When her master goes to bed at night, Kristi plops down on the floor right beside her bed. She will be there until her master arises.

Indeed, if Kristi loses track of her master for even one moment, she is obsessed with finding her again. Such restlessness is a sight to behold. Her nose is lifted; she agitatedly races from room to room until she finds her master again. When she finds her there is an explosion of joy that canine muscles and sinew can barely contain.

What disappointments, frustration, and pain Christians could be spared if they were as careful to keep Christ in view, to follow Him, and to be satisfied only when near Him. If, having lost Him, even for a moment, they were consumed with such a relentless pursuit of His presence, there would be far less backsliding.

Kristi maintains a steady devotion because *she is not distracted with secondary loyalties*. You see Kristi loves me too, but she has only *one master*. When we've been away and return, it's easy to see who she's most delighted to see. She rushes right past me and everyone else in the family to her master's side, and there it is again—that explosion of joy!

Kristi loves to romp and play, and she loves to eat, but she likes to have her master nearby. She keeps one eye on her food and one eye on her master. If her master gets too far away, she trots back and forth, stringing a few pellets along the way. She just can't bear to lose sight of her master.

The lesson for disciples here is simple. Love Jesus best of all—better than job, better than pleasure, better even than family. There can be no secondary loyalties disturbing one's dominant devotion.

Kristi's devotion is also demonstrated by *a supreme desire to please her master.* Nothing makes her happier than to hear the words, "Yes, you're a good dog," spoken with that special tender tone that dogs like to be affirmed with. If Kristi does something only "naughty dogs" do, however, her canine self-image sinks to its lowest level and is obvious to all. If there is ever a time when she doesn't want to see her master's face, this is it. Sometimes when she's been especially ugly, she even slinks off and hides.

Disobedience in a disciple works very much the same. No wonder Adam and Eve hid themselves. On the other hand, can anything compare with the consciousness of our Master's approval?

Most of the time Kristi's devotion is characterized by *instant and complete obedience.* She listens to her master's voice and commands. She loves to be put on a leash, to heel, to come, to fetch, to follow, to stay. To Kristi, there is no bondage in the *leash*—only liberty and the joy of pleasing. As disciples, we must view the Lord's leash as a means of experiencing His perfect plan for our lives.

Kristi has demonstrated a devotion that is fine-tuned, also. She studies her master's face. Those keen, intelligent Shepherd eyes scrutinize every expression. She responds even to her master's moods. It is not difficult to understand how a dog can detect distress and will protect its master.

*Kristi's devotion is undying.* We have no doubt that Kristi would fight to the death to protect her master. One canine authority writing on this breed said, "In relation to man he does not give affection lightly; he has plenty of dignity and some suspicion of strangers, but his friendship once given is given for life."

Devotion so illustrated has ignited a new flame of prayer in our hearts: "Lord, give us the kind of devotion exhibited by Kristi—deep, undisturbed, and undying devotion for You. Let it be the axis upon which all else in our lives turns. Let us be suspicious of anything that seeks to disturb that devotion. Amen."

## What Does a Disciple's Fruit Look Like?

We have learned that successful discipleship is a product of *relationship,* and that the relationship is maintained by love and obedience and keeping focused upon Jesus. It is worthy of note that God speaks about the "fruit of the Spirit." Discipleship is successful when our lives bear fruit. It is the indwelling Christ (The Holy Spirit is the Spirit of Christ) that produces fruit in our lives, thus the fruit of a disciple is clearly to be like Christ, and Galatians 5 spells out the components of that portrait.

"But the fruit of the Spirit is love, joy, peace, patience, kindness, goodness, faithfulness, gentleness, and self-control. Against such things there is no law. Those who belong to Christ Jesus have crucified the sinful nature with its passions and desires" (Gal. 5:22, 23).

And the Apostle also tells us what the fruit of the sinful nature are, so that we can recognize them and avoid them: "the acts of the sinful nature are obvious: sexual immorality, impurity, and debauchery; idolatry and witchcraft; hatred, discord, jealousy, fits of rage, selfish ambition, dissensions, factions, and envy; drunkenness, orgies and the like" And the Apostle affixes a firm warning to these acts: "I warn you, as I did before, that those who live like this will not inherit the kingdom of God" (Gal. 5:19–21).

David McKenna, expounding upon the fruit which our lives bear, says, "A culture that judges worth by the "bottom line" finds little value in these spiritual virtues (the fruit of the Spirit). *Consequences*, not character, become the basis for judgment. To achieve our utilitarian ends, the fruits of Machiavelli—hatred, hostility, discontent, impatience, toughness, aggression, skepticism, competiveness and intemperance—are better known to us than the fruits of the Spirit."[5]

McKenna also says, "The fruit of faith is revealed in our 'being' before it is demonstrated in our 'doing.' As there is danger in faith without works, there is also danger in works without faith. Because our society is geared to the 'bottom line,' focused on 'outcomes' and fixed on 'accountability,' we may err or the side of 'doing' rather than 'being.'" And McKenna warns, "The danger is to become driven by consequences and attuned to the Machiavellian fruits of hatred rather than love, happiness rather than joy, anxiety rather than peace, impatience rather than long-suffering, toughness rather than faith, aggression rather than meekness, and violence rather than temperance."[6]

"Fruit," according to Bonhoeffer, "is always the miraculous, the created; it is never the result of willing, but always a growth. The fruit of the Spirit is a gift of God, and only He can produce it . . . the saints are unconscious of the fruit they bear."[7]

Finally, McKenna wisely points out that "Christian maturity is shown in a balance between the fruits of our faith and the fruits of our works. Either one is an indicator of our spiritual growth, but in combination they become an unmatched distinctive of the Christian life."[8]

## The Spirit of Servanthood

Discipleship is successful when I am more interested in serving others than in being served. Certainly, as in everything else, Jesus is our most worthy model here. Jesus said, "the Son of Man did not come to be served, but to serve, and to give his life a ransom for many" (Mt. 20:28).

His whole life was one of sacrificial service given for others. The Apostle Paul spoke of this spirit that characterized our Lord, "who being in very nature God, did not consider equality with God something to be grasped, but *made himself nothing, taking the very nature of a servant*; being made in human likeness. And being found in appearance as a man, he humbled himself and became obedient to death—even death on a cross" (Phil. 2:6–8).

Who could forget that most touching of scenes when Jesus took a towel and a basin of water and washed His disciples feet— the Son of God stooping to serve His followers and all mankind. The spirit of servanthood has characterized Christ's followers in every age. William Barclay believed that growth in servanthood means becoming 1) inalienably possessed by God, 2) unqualifiedly at the disposal of God, 3) unquestionably obedient to God, and 4) constantly in the service of God.[9]

Perhaps one of the greatest modern-day examples of servanthood is that of Mother Teresa and her work. "When Mother Teresa picked up that first dying woman from a Calcutta street, a barely recognizable scrap Yof humanity, soiled by dirt and spittle, she did not know that this rescue would be the first of thousands upon thousands. In the coming decades an unending line of desolate human beings would need to be saved from dying like animals in the gutter."[10]

This was only one of the acts of sacrificial servanthood that expressed Mother Teresa's vision of the dignity and glory of each person's worth. No wonder she was awarded the Nobel Peace prize. We can't all be Mother Teresas, but we should all have that same spirit.

Mother Teresa put it this way: "The streets of Calcutta lead to everyone's door, and the very pain, the very ruin of our Calcutta is the hearts witness to the glory that once was. I know you think you should make a trip to Calcutta, but I strongly advise you to save your airfare and spend it on the poor in your own country. It is easy to love people far away. It is not always easy to love those who live right next to us. There are thousands of people dying for a piece of bread. There are thousands more dying for a little bit of love, for a little bit of acknowlegement."[11]

## Discipleship and the Inward Testimony

Discipleship can only be called successful if we have an inward testimony that we belong to Christ and that our lives please Him. The Apostle John gave us some clear criteria for evaluating our credibility as Christians. He wrote: "We know that we have come to know Him (Jesus) if we obey his commands. The man who says, 'I know him,' but does not do what he commands is a liar and the truth is not in him. But if anyone obeys his word, God's love is truly made complete in him. This is how we know we are in him: *whoever claims to live in him must walk as Jesus did*" (1 Jn. 2:3–6, emphasis mine).

Furthermore, John, who has been called the Apostle of Love, has made it clear that a life that pleases God will be defined by love. John wrote: "Dear friends, since God so loved us, we ought to love one another. No one has ever seen God, but if we love one another, God lives in us and his love is made complete in us" (1 Jn. 4:11,12).

John emphasized that "anyone who claims to be in the light but hates his brother is still in darkness. Whoever loves his brother lives in the light . . . (1 Jn. 2:9,10) and "if we walk in the light as He (Jesus) is in the light we have fellowship with one another and the blood of Jesus His Son, purifies us from all sin" (1 Jn. 1:7).

Successful discipleship is not something that we can non-arbitrarily judge about another, but for ourselves it must at least involve a vital relationship with Jesus that results in the "fruit of the Spirit" and "the spirit of servanthood," both of which are the result of staying connected to and focused upon Jesus our heavenly Vine, and both of which are the product of His divine love at work in and through us.

Discipleship is successful when my daily life rings true to my testimony. In *Pilgrim's Progress*, Christian, commenting upon "Talkative's" character said, "His house is as empty of religion as the white of an egg is of savor. There is there neither prayer nor sign of repentance for sin; yea, the brute in his kind serves God far better than he. He is the very stain, reproach, and shame of religion to all that know him—saint abroad, and a devil at home."[12]

Keith Phillips says, "The indispensable evidence in discerning whether you are a spiritual version of fool's gold or the real thing is the presence of a Christ-like character. If Christ's character is missing, you have not died to yourself and are not fit for reproduction."[13]

But no journey is ultimately successful that does not reach its destination. In the next chapter we will seek to discover where this road of discipleship leads a follower of Jesus.

# QUESTIONS FOR REFLECTION

1. What are some of the criteria by which the secular world judges success?

2. Should Christian disciples employ these same criteria in evaluating the success of their discipleship?

3. What forms the "core" of successful discipleship?

4. What Biblical metaphor best illustrates this core?

5. What word, used repetitively by Jesus in John 15, describes the "essential" for bearing fruit in our Christian lives?

6. Describe Jesus' relationship with His Father. What three things characterize that relationship?

7. How does the German Shepherd dog, Kristi, provide a window on successful discipleship?

8. How does the late Mother Teresa and her work throw light upon the concept of successful discipleship?

# A PRAYER FOR SERIOUS FOLLOWERS

Father, don't let me judge the success of my Christian discipleship and service by this world's standards. May my focus and concentration be forever upon Jesus and my relationship to Him.

Help me to stay connected to Jesus, my heavenly Vine, so that I can bear the fruit of the Spirit.

Father, let me be to Jesus all that Jesus was to You, so that Jesus can be to me all that You were to your Son. Let me faithfully serve you in the spirit of love and true obedience, allowing you to judge my life and work. In Jesus' name, Amen.

# CHAPTER FOURTEEN

# WHERE DOES THIS ROAD LEAD?

*Within the life of every Christian, then there has begun that progressive Godly process that will bring him into the wideness of eternity qualified for the presence of God and sweetly enabled to serve with Him in the infinite reaches of heaven.*

—Dave Breese

*There is an endless kingdom to be inhabited; and everlasting life to be given us, that we may inhabit that kingdom forever . . . there are crowns of glory to be given us; and garments that will make us shine like the sun in the firmament of heaven.*

—"Christian" in *Pilgrim's Progress*

*Securities belie their name. Banks and insurance companies will pass away. Precious metals have all through history been stolen. There is no such thing on earth as a safe investment—not even a "fairly" safe one. But heavenly treasure is guaranteed by the name of Jehovah.*

—Dietrich Bonhoeffer

We have been on "Discipleship Road" these past thirteen chapters. Quite likely you have already personally experienced many blessings in following Jesus. Hopefully this handbook on discipleship has either helped you to get on that road, or to discover how "to stay on that road."

There is a reason why we want that to happen, for you see, a road is a "path" or a "highway," or a "route" to a *destination*. The "road of discipleship" is going *somewhere*. It is a journey with an end in view.

The destination is the reward, but the journey itself is a blessed reward also. It is not just a "treadmill" to exercise one's spiritual lungs and heart, although it does that. The road of discipleship leads to a definite destiny—a recognizable reward.

When God called Abraham (Abram, as he was first called), to leave his country, his people, and his father's household, to go to a "land I will show you," He was promising him a definite geographical place on this planet. But God was promising much more than that.

God was promising a "reward of blessing." "I will bless you and make your name great. You will be a blessing. I will bless those who bless you and curse those who curse you. All the people on earth will be blessed through you" (Gen. 12:1–3).

Clearly, God is offering to Abraham a spiritual blessing, but it is a blessing with tangible rewards in this world and this life, and with implications of reward in a life and world to come. *The road of discipleship leads to both an earthly destination or reward and a heavenly destination and reward.*

Jesus said, "I tell you the truth, no one who has left home or wife or brothers or parents or children for the sake of the kingdom of God will fail to receive many times as much in this age and, in the age to come, eternal life" (Lk. 18:29, 30). When we travel "Discipleship Road" we are journeying toward a place of incomparable earthly reward and a place of eternal and supernal heavenly blessings. The Christian life gives us both a "reason to live," and a "reason to die." The value of *discipleship* is that it equips us for both earth and heaven. In this chapter, we want to look briefly at these rewards.

## Discipleship Leads to Incomparable Earthly Reward

What exactly are the earthly rewards of following Jesus in faithful discipleship? First, **to know Jesus**. The road of discipleship is the road to Jesus. Could there be a better reward than simply to *know Jesus intimately*? To know Him better? To learn from Him? To love Him with all the heart, mind, and soul? St. Francis said to his dying mother, "I thank you for having given me life. When I think it through, it has all been a single road to God."[1]

The Apostle Paul said, "I consider everything loss compared to the surpassing greatness of *knowing Christ Jesus my Lord* . . . I want to know Christ and the power of his resurrection" (Phil. 3:8, 10, emphasis mine).

J. I. Packer asks, "What were we made for? To know God. What aim should we set for ourselves in life? To know God. What is the 'eternal life' that Jesus gives? Knowledge of God—'this is life eternal, that they might know thee, the only true God, and Jesus Christ whom thou has sent' (Jn. 17:3). What is the best thing in life, bringing more joy, delight, and contentment, than anything else? Knowledge of God."[2]

> "My goal is God Himself, not joy, nor peace, Nor even blessing, but Himself, my God; Tis His to lead me there, not mine, but His—At any cost, dear Lord, by any road!"[3]
>
> —F. Brook

Jesus was always watching His Father, and listening to His Father, and seeking to know and do His Father's will. Obviously Jesus knew there was great benefit in *knowing* His Father. When we are prepared to do the same with Jesus—to really know Him—Jesus will be to us all that His Father was to Him.

Packer explains what knowing God involves: "first, listening to God's Word and receiving it as the Holy Spirit interprets it, in application to oneself; second, noting God's nature and character, as His Word and works reveal it; third, accepting His invitations, and doing what He commands; fourth, recognizing, and rejoicing in, the love that He has shown to us."[4]

Packer could just as well have defined discipleship here. *The first and greatest reward of discipleship will always be simply to discover the incomparable treasure that is Jesus.* To know Him is to love Him. To love Him is to obey Him. And to obey Him is to have the testimony that our lives please Him, and to learn to know Him even better.

Packer would sum up this earthly reward of "knowing Jesus," this way: "The world becomes a strange, mad, painful place, and life in it a disappointing and unpleasant business for those who do not know God. Disregard the study of God, and you sentence yourself to stumble and blunder through life blindfold, as it were, with no sense of direction and no understanding of what surrounds you. This way you can waste your life and lose your soul."[5]

A second earthly reward of discipleship can be stated succinctly: *The better we know Christ the greater our trust in Him.* Two things Jesus marveled at when He was here on earth was *faith* and *lack of faith*. Faith is a personal trust in the person of the Savior.

Discipleship is the path to that personal trust. Discipleship forges a relationship between the disciple and the Lord that not only strengthens one's spiritual life, but makes it easier for one to glorify the Lord.

That leads to a third earthly reward of discipleship—*the reward of reflecting Christ better.* The ancient creed said, "The chief end of man is to glorify God and to enjoy Him forever." Discipleship provides a double-barreled reward—knowing and enjoying Christ better and reflecting His glory better. The better we know Christ (not just *about* Him) the more of His image we will shine into the world and the better we serve the Master.

## Discipleship Leads to a Place of Eternal and Supernal Blessing

Discipleship Road leads to great blessings in this life, but *this life is not all there is, folks.* Not for the Christian, nor for the non-Christian. The road of discipleship leads not only to incomparable earthly blessings, but to heavenly rewards.

This fallen world could never provide or contain the reward God has for those who love Him and follow His Son through this life. It will take a *new world* for that—and that is exactly what God has promised us—*A New World.*

The Apostle John said, "Then I saw a new heaven and a new earth, for the first heaven and the first earth had passed away" (Rev. 21:1). It is well to keep in mind that God is not a "patcher-upper." God's reward for His faithful followers will not be just the old present world, worked over a bit. It will be entirely new!

And if you enjoy church and God's people here on earth, get ready for the "superlative worship experience" in heaven. John said, "And I heard a great voice out of heaven saying, Behold the tabernacle of God is with men, and he will dwell with them and they shall be his people, and God himself shall be with them and be their God" (v. 3, KJV).

The Old Testament "tabernacle" was an archetype of the place where God and man meet. Jesus Himself was God incarnate, tabernacling with man in this present world order, and this verse also is a glimpse of the final, eternal and supernal tabernacling of God with men in the last day.

It is significant that the first and principal focus of John's revelation of heaven is of God and man *together.* Isn't that what the entire unfolding drama of redemption is about—*God and man together* in eternal reconciliation and relationship?

In this "tabernacling" we see what makes heaven the rich reward it will be. As J. I. Packer writes: "What will make heaven to be heaven is the presence of Jesus, and of a reconciled divine Father who loves us for Jesus' sake no less than He loves Jesus Himself. To see, and know, and love, and be loved by the Father and the Son, in company with the rest of God's vast family, is the whole essence of the Christian's hope."[6] John MacArthur put it this way: "The presence of Christ is what makes heaven *heaven* . . . and perfect fellowship with God is the very essence of heaven."[7]

But God's revelation to John gives us many other details about heaven. We are told that "God shall wipe away all tears from their eyes; and there shall be no more death, neither sorrow, nor crying, neither shall there be any more pain: for the former things are passed away. And He that sat upon the throne said, Behold I make all things new" (Rev. 21:4, 5, KJV).

Richard Baxter writes: "In heaven danger and trouble is over; there is nothing but what will advance our joy. As we rest from temptations, so also from all the abuses and persecutions which we suffer in the hands of wicked men."[8] In the long path trod by the followers of Jesus through the 2000 years past, many have been persecuted, tortured, and killed for their faith. Even today there is an ugly side often hidden. In the last few days I received a letter from Wycliffe Associates explaining that in an area too politically sensitive to be named, twenty-three Bible translation facilities and homes—the work of two decades—were burned to the ground.[9]

But, this is all going to end. In heaven, as Baxter writes, "We shall be scorned, derided, imprisoned, banished, butchered by them no more . . . this is the time for crowning with thorns, buffeting, spitting on; that (heaven) will be the time for crowning with glory. . . . Now we must be hated of all men for Christ's sake, and the gospel; then will Christ be admired in His saints. . . . Now as they hated Christ, they will also hate us, then, as they will honor Christ, so will they also honor us . . . nor is truth clothed in robes of error

. . . and a saint found bleeding, nor our friends smite us, mistaking us for their enemies. There is none of this blind, mad work there."[10]

MacArthur, succinctly sums up the environment of heaven this way: "Murphy's law will finally be nullified. In heaven whatever might go wrong can't."[11] The final and ultimate destiny of the road of discipleship will be better than we can ever imagine and better than we deserve. Don't worry if you can't imagine a city whose streets are gold and whose gates are of Pearl. Remember, this is a *new order* of things.

The gold and pearl may be literal, but it may be as Ralph Earle says, "all these materials that are mentioned are to be taken symbolically, in keeping with the nature of the Book of Revelation. What we have here is an attempt to describe the indescribable. Finite language is inadequate for portraying the Infinite. John does his best to picture the superlative beauties of the next life. It should whet our eagerness for Christ to come and bring in the new order."[12]

Are you on Discipleship Road? Are you on the road to your reward? Christians are often accused of being "pie-in-the-sky" people. The meaning of that is to imply that they are so fascinated and occupied with the thought of heaven that they are of no earthly use. I suppose it is possible for one to have so much preoccupation with the next world—the heavenly reward—as to find little joy, reward, or usefulness in this one.

However, my experience has taught me that the greater danger by far for Christians is to be so *earthly minded*—so occupied with this world's materialism and the cares of this world that they disqualify themselves for their heavenly reward.

The final words of the book of Revelation reveal the heartbeat of God—His deep concern and love for the unsaved. "And the Spirit and the bride say, 'Come,' and let him who hears say 'come!' Whoever is thirsty, let him come; and whoever wishes, let him take the free gift of the water of life" (Rev. 22:17).

These words not only let us see the great heart of God, but they keep us reminded of the whole purpose of discipleship—not only to become overcomers by finishing our own race, but to make disciples of all nations as Jesus commanded (Mt. 28:19). The reward will be worth the cost—not only for us, but for all whom we can get to make the journey with us.

This is a very limited treatment of God's prepared and waiting reward for His faithful followers. There is no way we can give it adequate treatment in the scope of this book, but as John MacArthur says, "Scripture repeatedly makes clear that heaven is a realm of unsurpassed joy, unfading glory, undiminished bliss, unlimited delights, and unending pleasures. Nothing about it can possibly be boring or humdrum. It will be a perfect existence."[13]

Heaven is real and it is the reward of all those who follow Jesus in faithful discipleship. As John Piper says, "God will spend eternity exhausting the treasures of His immeasurable grace on us."[14] Even this figure of speech breaks down for God's riches are not exhaustible even on us. This is our destiny. Stay on the "road."

But will God's grace be good enough to see us through to the finish line? In the next and final chapter we take a look at just how good God's grace is.

## QUESTIONS FOR REFLECTION

1. Discuss what the author means when he says the road of discipleship is going "somewhere."?

2. What are at least three "earthly" rewards of discipleship?

3. How does the Old Testament concept of "tabernacling" relate to the eternal reward for finishing the race of discipleship?

4.   What is it that makes heaven *heaven*?

5.   What did John MacArthur mean when he said of heaven that "Murphy's law" will finally be nullified?

6.   What do you think is the greater danger: to be too *heavenly minded* or to be too *earthly minded*?

7.   Does the Bible devote much space to a Christian's final destiny?

## A PRAYER FOR SERIOUS FOLLOWERS

Lord, there are inexorable joys in just being on the journey of Christian discipleship. The first and greatest reward will always be simply to discover the inescapable treasure that is You—my Jesus.

Thank you for taking me deeper into the exquisite pleasure which can be found only in intimate relationship with You.

Ah, but never let me forget, dear Jesus, that there is a new world coming, called heaven. Only in that place can God's ultimate reward for faithful discipleship be experienced. Only then and there will your children be able to enjoy unsurpassed joy and unfading glory.

Help me, Lord, to stay on the road that leads to this eternal bliss. In your precious name, Amen.

# CHAPTER FIFTEEN

# WILL GOD'S GRACE BE GOOD ENOUGH?

*And God is able to make all grace abound to you, so that in all things at all times, having all that you need, you will abound in every good work.*

*—2 Corinthians 9:8*

*If God is for us, who can be against us? He who did not spare his own Son, but gave Him up for us all—how will He not also give us all things?*

*—Romans 8:32*

*For I am convinced that neither death nor life, neither angels, nor demons, neither the present nor the future, nor any powers, neither height, nor depth, nor anything else in all creation, will be able to separate us from the love of God that is in Christ Jesus our Lord.*

*—Romans 8:38,39*

In this consumer-oriented age, we tend to think in terms of product quality and service. So, if you are a follower of Jesus or you are considering becoming His disciple, you may be wondering about this product called *grace*? Will it be good enough to keep me in my journey of discipleship?

Years ago a certain oil company claimed its product was "better than it has to be." The claim implied that it's motor oil not only provided the lubrication and protection expected, but assured the consumer of additives and extras that made it a superior product.

If a product is ever really better than it has to be, that is a very good testimony to its worth. A local television station runs a segment where various product claims are put to the test by consumers. After using the product for some time, the consumers rate the product according to how it lived up to the manufacturer's claims. Rarely, it seems, does a product really get top marks.

We live in an age when "just getting by" seems to be good enough. Few companies or individuals are willing to give that extra effort which assures excellence of performance, craftsmanship, and service. Mediocrity reigns. But what about this thing we call "grace"?

What can I count on as a disciple of Christ? Clearly I've got to do *my* part. That should be obvious from the previous chapters of this book, but can God be counted on to do *His* part? Will *grace* be adequate? Are there any "extras"? Any "additives"?

## God's Grace—Better Than It Has to Be

Extravagant claims are not uncommon in modern advertising, but the claims of the gospel of Jesus Christ are not excessive. God's grace is indeed *better than it has to be*. Its claims are never deceptive or extravagant. God's grace offers prodigality of product, performance, and service.

God's grace must be good enough to save us from the *penalty* of sin—both the final penalty of everlasting punishment and separation from God, and the present penalty of alienation from God, and the haunting ghost of guilt. This "saving" includes the sovereign act of "forgiveness"—God, for Christ's sake, forgives all our past sins. Amazing peace comes to the one to whom Christ says, "Your sins are forgiven."

Furthermore, this "saving" provides *justification*—God's judicial act of treating us "just as if we had never sinned." Is that good grace, or what? But God still isn't through. That part of grace—forgiving and justifying—is significant enough, but it might not be fully satisfying and enduring were it not for a complimentary aspect of grace called by theologians—*regeneration*. This is the renewal of our fallen nature by the power of the Holy Spirit. Spiritual life and power lost as a result of the Fall, are regenerated in the human soul.

But, say, God's grace isn't finished yet. There is a "parental" aspect of this "saving grace" also. This is where God treats us with "family" love. We are adopted into the family of God. Although we were alienated from God and strangers to His grace, God treats us as sons and daughters and heirs of all He has.

## A Work of Grace Co-extensive with the Work of Sin

Pretty good product, wouldn't you say? Could there be more? Yes, there is even more. God's grace is pervasive and thorough. God wants to cleanse our hearts from the very presence and power of *sinfulness*. He wants to deliver us from the root and "tyranny" of sin.

John the Baptist said, "I baptize you with water for repentance. But after me will come one who is more powerful than I, whose sandals I am not fit to carry. He will baptize you with the Holy Spirit and with fire. His winnowing fork is in his hand, and he will clear his threshing floor, gathering his wheat into the barn and burning up the chaff with unquenchable fire" (Mt. 3:11, 12).

Commissioner S. L. Brengle of the Salvation Army, wrote: "The great hindrance in the hearts of God's children to the power of the Holy Ghost is inbred sin—that dark, defiant, evil something within that struggles for the mastery of the soul, and will not submit to be the meek and lowly and patient and forbearing and holy as was Jesus; and when the Holy Spirit comes, His first work is to sweep away that something, that carnal principle, and make free and clean all the channels of the soul."[1]

And another great Salvation Army soul, Dr. Samuel Chadwick, put it this way: "As pardon abounds over guilt so sanctification abounds over the presence of sin in the soul. Forgiveness without cleansing would not cover man's need. The work of grace must be co-extensive with the work of sin. Where sin had its seat His throne is established. The will is surrendered, the heart cleansed, the desire changed and the nature renewed. Sin disturbed the true order of man's nature and defaced the divine image within him. Grace creates him anew after the image of God in righteousness and true holiness. No man need continue in sin, for grace has abounded unto complete salvation."[2]

What we are trying to establish is that God's grace is more than adequate for all our needs. God's grace is more than a "rescue squad," or a "life-support system." It does more than save us and then barely keep us alive. God's grace can make a radical change in the core of our being and can furnish purpose and power for everyday life. God integrates the personality and frees it to function at its intended norm. He releases us from the delusion of self-reliance, yet never crushes the individual free spirit.

God's grace is always better than it has to be. As with the water and fire on Mount Carmel, God has more than enough to vindicate His holy name. Whether it is a barrel of meal that does not waste or a cruse of oil that never fails, God's grace is not diminished, and His account is never embarrassed by our draw upon it.

## God's Grace Is Like a Spring

Biblical images of God's grace as a *spring* abound. Jesus said to the Samaritan woman, "whoever drinks the water I give him will never thirst. Indeed, the water I give him will become in him a spring of water welling up to eternal life" (Jn. 4:14). Springs have played a valuable role in the survival of man.

The story of how the Cherokee Indians were driven from their homeland in the Eastern Highlands of the United States and moved halfway across the continent is well known. Their journey in the fall and winter of 1838–39 is a bittersweet drama known as the "Trail of Tears." More than 4,000 died along the way from disease, hunger, and exposure.

There is another saga of sadness that comes to mind. It began with the tragic story of man's displacement from his "garden" home in the beginning of human history. The Cherokees probably did nothing to deserve their suffering, but man's eviction from the Garden was the direct result of his disobedience and sin. Sin always leaves a trail of tears.

But history records that the Cherokees spent one week of their year-long journey camped by the beautiful Blue Spring near Eureka Springs, Arkansas. The "Trail of Tears" half encircles the spring, which is today just as it was when the Cherokees used it. The spring flows from an unknown depth, and according to geologists, the water is of glacier origin and comes from the Pacific Northwest by way of an underground river. The official capacity of the spring is given as 38 million gallons every 24 hours.

Just as the "Trail of Tears" reminds one of the works of the devil, nature's Blue Spring is an apt illustration of the Holy Spirit and God's grace. The Spirit provides man with an unparalleled quality of life, flowing from a great hidden source in eternity.

The depth of grace has never been sounded, and the supply is inexhaustible.

Water has always been a precious commodity to man. His villages and cities have been built near rivers, lakes, and springs. Archeological excavations, as well as secular and biblical history, reveal the existence of waterworks for the procuring, purifying, and storing of water in ancient cultures.

Arkansas' Blue Spring may have been one of few refreshing spots along the Cherokee's Trail of Tears." No doubt they wished they could take it with them when they were forced to march on. While man has often had to leave his earthly water supplies behind, *God has planned it that His disciples will have a perpetual spring of spiritual life welling up within them.* They never have to leave it behind. The spring is not just good enough, but better than it has to be.

## God's River of Grace Runs Full

There is ample evidence in God's Word that our sovereign Lord also works with *fullness.* The psalmist said, "The streams of God are filled with water" (Ps. 65:9). Or, as the King James Version reads, "The river of God runs full." The meaning is that God's provision is one of *fullness.*

Having known the Arkansas River in northeast Oklahoma, it was a big surprise when we pastored in Dodge City, Kansas, to find the Arkansas River bed dry. It wasn't always that way, but Colorado had damned up the river and only when their reservoirs were running too full from the melting of heavy snows would one find water in the river bed.

Each of our lives is a riverbed through which God wants to allow His mighty grace to flow. That grace—the water of life—is born in the virgin snows of God's sovereign holiness. That water will cleanse from pollution and will refresh and satisfy the thirsty soul. God has an ample supply of water, but very often there are things in our lives that have the supply of grace damned up.

A dry riverbed is not very pretty. Without the river of God running full through any life, things quickly begin to droop and die. Drought and barrenness and infertility result. But water means *life.*

In the early days of our country, the old mills were vital for providing power for grinding corn, and powering saws, etc. When the mill shut down, the miller would gather together the people of the community and they would go upstream and clean out the tree limbs and rubbish that had collected and damned up the stream so that they could get the mills running again.

It is the same in the disciple's life or the life of the church. When the water is not running full, we need to ask what has happened to damn up the free flowing of God's grace in our lives? Is it sin or disobedience of any kind? Is it unforgiveness or resentment? Is it neglect of God's Word or of prayer? What will it take to get the streams of God running full through our lives? God said, "I will make rivers flow on barren heights, and springs within the valleys. I will turn the desert into pools of water, and the parched ground into springs (Isa. 41:18).

When Colorado opened the floodgates at the dams, and water began to come down the Arkansas, in Dodge City, people got excited. Even a small stream of water stirred interest. One could hear them say things like, "Have you been out to see the water?" or "It looks good to see water in the riverbed again." Just so, when the disciples of Jesus open the riverbed of their lives to God's grace, people will take notice. People will get excited and thirsty.

God wants more than a trickle of grace running through His disciples' lives though, for God always works in fullness. His grace is good enough and better than it has to be. But each disciple decides whether or not the river will run full in his or her own life.

## An Apostle's Prayer for Disciples

The apostle Paul wrote: "And God is able to make all grace abound to you, so that in all things at all times, having all that you need, you will abound in every good work." (2 Cor. 9:8) God's grace is good enough for every disciple in every circumstance in any age, including the new century and millennium. I can count on it! Can God count on me?

The Apostle's prayer for those first-century followers of Jesus surely encouraged their faithful discipleship. He would as readily pray that prayer for you and me:

"I pray that out of his glorious riches he may strengthen you with power through his Spirit in your inner being, so that Christ may dwell in your hearts through faith. And I pray that you, being rooted and established in love, may have power together with all saints, to grasp how wide and long and high and deep Is the love of Christ, and to know this love that surpasses knowledge—That you may be filled to the measure of all the fullness of God. Now to him who is able to do immeasurably more than all we ask or imagine, according to his power that is at work within us, to him be glory in the church and in Christ Jesus throughout all generations, for ever and ever. Amen."

—Eph. 3:16–21

# QUESTIONS FOR REFLECTION

1. In this consumer-oriented age, what are some things we think about in regard to a product?

2. In the spiritual realm, is it legitimate to ask questions about God's product of grace, salvation, and preservation?

3. In what way is God's grace better than it has to be? Discuss this in relation to sin, guilt, cleansing, keeping power, etc.?

4. In what way is God's grace like a Spring?

5. Explain what God and the author mean by the Biblical declaration : "The river of God runs full."

6. What do I personally need to do to keep the river of grace running full through my life?

# A PRAYER FOR SERIOUS FOLLOWERS

O'God, you have never called anyone to an assignment and failed to adequately equip them for the task. Thank you for calling me to be your disciple. I am learning how wide, and long, and high, and deep is your love and grace. Your grace is better than it has to be.

I long to be filled to the measure of all the fullness of God. Let there be in me that deep Blue Spring Jesus spoke of in John 7, and help me to always keep the rubbish and trash out of the riverbed of my life so the river of Your grace can run full and overflow.

Thank you for giving to me *starting* grace, *daily keeping* grace, and *finishing* grace. In Jesus' name, Amen.

# NOTES

**Introduction**

[1] Oswald Chambers, *If Thou Wilt Be Perfect* (Ft. Washington: Christian Literature Crusade, 1973), p. 106.
[2] Dallas Willard, *The Spirit of the Disciplines* (San Francisco: Harper Collins, 1988), pp. 260–1.
[3] William A. Dembski, ed., *Mere Creation* (Downers Grove: Inter-Varsity Press, 1998), p. 13.
[4] Willard, *Spirit of Disciplines, p. 258.*
[5] Elton Trueblood, *The Company of the Committed* (New York: Harper and Row Publishers, 1961), p. 17.
[6] Elton Trueblood, *Alternatives to Futility* (Waco: Word Books, 1948), p. 61.
[7] Ronald J. Sider, *Living Like Jesus* (Grand Rapids: Baker Books, 1996), p. 16.
[8] Judson Jerome, *The Poet and the Poem* (Cincinnati: Writer's Digest Books, 1979), p. 351.

**Chapter One**

[1] Oswald Chambers, *If Thou Wilt Be Perfect* (Ft. Washington: Christian Literature Crusade, 1973), p. 104, emphasis mine.
[2] Dietrich Bonhoeffer, *The Cost of Discipleship* (New York: Macmillan Publishing Co., 1979), p. 105.
[3] Dave Breese, *Discover Your Destiny* (Waco: Word Books, 1965), p. 94
[4] Bonhoeffer, *Cost*, pp. 73, 76, emphasis mine.
[5] J. Heinrich Arnold, *Discipleship: Living for Christ in the Daily Grind* (Farmington: The Plough Publishing House, 1994), p. 53, emphasis mine.

[6] Oswald Chambers, *Not Knowing Whither* (*Basingstoke*: Marshall, Morgan, & Scott, 1975) p. 61.

[7] Bonhoeffer, *Cost*, pp. 70, 76

[8] George A. Buttrick, "Our Call and Cross," *The Gift of Easter*, ed. Floyd Thatcher (Waco: Word Books, 1976), p. 136.

[9] Bonhoeffer, *Cost, p. 68.*

[10] Bruce L. Shelley, *Church History in Plain Language* (*Waco*: Word Books, 1982), p. 30, emphasis mine.

[11] Rob L. Staples, *Outward Sign and Inward Grace* (*Kansas* City: Beacon Hill Press, 1991), p. 146.

[12] H. Orton Wiley, *Christian Theology V. 3* (*Kansas* City: Beacon Hill Press, 1943), p. 175.

[13] Staples, *Outward Sign*, pp. 124, 130.

[14] Staples, *Outward Sign,* p. 120.

[15] Becky Benenate & Joseph Durepos, *Mother Teresa: No Greater Love* (*Novato*: New World Library, 1997), p. 54.

[16] Henry Blackaby & Claude King, *Experiencing God* (*Nashville*: Broadman & Holman Publishers, 1994), pp. 25, 26.

[17] Benenate, *Mother Teresa, pp. 83,84.*

[18] Lewis B. Smedes, *Mere Morality* (*Grand* Rapids: Wm. B. Eerdmans Publishing Co., 1983), p. viii.

[19] Bonhoeffer, *Cost,* p. 41.

[20] Breese, *Discover Your Destiny*, p. 95.

**Chapter Two**

[1] Dallas Willard, *The Spirit of the Disciplines* (San Francisco: Harper Collins, 1988), p. 258.

[2] Greg Laurie, *Discipleship: The Next Step in Following Jesus* (Eugene: Harvest House, 1993), p. 5.

[3] Willard, *Spirit of Disciplines, p. 23.*

[4] Ronald J. Sider, *Living Like Jesus* (*Grand* Rapids: Baker Books, 1996), p. 11.

[5] Keith Phillips, *The Making of a Disciple* (Old Tappan: Fleming H. Revell Company, 1981), p. 7.

[6] Sider, *Living Like Jesus, p. 34.*

[7] Sider, *Living Like Jesus.*

[8] Laurie, *Discipleship*, p. 9.

[9] Henry Blackaby & Claude King, *Experiencing God* (*Nashville*: Broadman & Holman Publishers, 1994), p. 96, emphasis mine.

[10] Dietrich Bonhoeffer, *The Cost of Discipleship* (*New* York: Macmillan Publishing Co., 1979), p. 62.

[11] Blackaby, *Experiencing God*, p. 250.

[12] E. Stanley Jones, *A Song of Ascents* (*Nashville*: Abingdon Festival Books, 1968), p. 21, emphasis mine.

13 J. Heinrich Arnold, *Discipleship: Living for Christ in the Daily Grind* (*Farmington*: The Plough Publishing House, 1994), p. 19.

14 Blackaby, *Experiencing God*, p. 35.

15 Oswald Chambers, *Not Knowing Whither* (*Basingstoke*: Marshall, Morgan, & Scott, 1975), pp. 11, 14.

16 Bonhoeffer, *Cost*, p. 62.

17 John Bunyan, *Pilgrim's Progress* (Grand Rapids: Zondervan, 1966), p. 13.

18 John White, *Magnificent Obsession* (Downer's Grove: Inter-Varsity Press, 1976), pp. 36–7.

19 Michael Molinos, *The Spiritual Guide* (Sargent: Seedsowers, 1972), p. 104.

20 Amy Carmichael, *Thou Givest—They Gather* (Ft. Washington: Christian Literature Crusade, 1971), p. 147.

21 Bonhoeffer, *Cost*, p. 63, emphasis mine.

22 Bonhoeffer, *Cost*, pp. 61–2.

23 Oswald Chambers, *If Thou Wilt Be Perfect* (Ft. Washington: Christian Literature Crusade, 1973), pp. 106–7.

24 Blackaby, *Experiencing God*, p. 109.

25 Douglas Groothuis, *The Soul in Cyberspace* (Grand Rapids: Baker Books, 1997), p. 87

**Chapter Three**

1 Oswald Chambers, *The Place of Help* (New York: Grosset & Dunlap, 1936), p. 159.

2 Dallas Willard, *The Spirit of the Disciplines* (*San* Francisco: Harper Collins, 1988), p. 14.

3 A. W. Tozer, *The Pursuit of God* (*Wheaton*: Tyndale House Publishers, 1982), p. 67.

4 Tozer, *Pursuit*, p. 69.

5 Douglas Groothuis, *The Soul in Cyberspace* (Grand Rapids: Baker Books, 1997), p. 162.

6 Tozer, *Pursuit*, p. 70.

7 Oswald Chambers, *Approved Unto God* (Grand Rapids: Discovery House Publishers, 1997), p. 70.

8 E. Stanley Jones, *The Christ of the Mount* (*Nashville*: Abingdon, 1981), p. 22.

9 Chambers, *Approved Unto God*, p. 71.

10 Oswald Chambers, *Studies in the Sermon on the Mount* (Ft. Washington: Christian Literature Crusade, 1960), p. 37.

11 Elizabeth Elliot, *Shadow of the Almighty* (*New* York: Harper & Brothers, 1958), p. 247.

12 Bruce L. Shelley, *Church History in Plain Language* (*Waco*: Word Books, 1982), p. 16.

13 Oswald Chambers, Approved Unto God, pp. 70,71.

[14] Elizabeth Elliot, ed, *The Journals of Jim Elliot* (Grand Rapids: Fleming H. Revell, 1978), pp. 215,16.

[15] Francis J. Roberts, *Come Away My Beloved* (Ojai: King's Farspan, Inc., 1970), pp. 30,31.

[16] Elliot, *Journals*, pp. 216,17.

[17] Tozer, *Pursuit*, p. 15.

[18] *Pursuit*, p. 11.

## Chapter Four

[1] Lloyd John Ogilvie, *Drumbeat of Love* (*Waco*: Word Books, 1976), P. 15.

[2] Oswald Chambers, *The Place of Help* (New York: Grosset & Dunlap Publishers, 1936), p. 203.

[3] A. J. Gordon, *The Ministry of the Spirit* (Minneapolis: Bethany House Publishers, 1985), p. 56, emphasis mine.

[4] W. T. Purkiser, *Interpreting Christian Holiness* (Kansas City: Beacon Hill Press, 1971), p. 15, emphasis mine.

[5] James Gilchrist Lawson, *Deeper Experiences of Famous Christians* (Anderson: Warner Press & Pyramid Publications, 1970), p. 8.

[6] Lawson, *Deeper Experiences*, p. 8.

[7] Lawson, *Deeper Experiences*, p. 9.

[8] Richard S. Taylor, *What Does It Mean to be Filled With the Spirit?* (Kansas City: Beacon Hill Press, 1995), p. 28.

[9] Taylor, *What Does it Mean?*, p. 63.

[10] Taylor, *What Does it Mean?*, p. 65.

[11] Ogilvie, *Drumbeat*, p. 82.

[12] Taylor, *What Does It Mean?*, p. 67.

[13] A. B. Simpson, *The Holy Spirit* (Harrisburg: Christian Publications, Inc., 1896), p. 89.

## Chapter Five

[1] A. Skevington Wood, *Life By The Spirit* (Grand Rapids: Zondervan Publishing House, 1964), p. 59.

[2] A. B. Simpson, *When the Comforter Came* (Harrisburg: Christian Publications, Inc., 1911), 13th day.

[3] Richard S. Taylor, *Life in the Spirit* (Kansas City: Beacon Hill Press, 1966), p. 109.

[4] C. S. Lewis, "Caring for People God's Way," *External Divisions Catalog*, American Association of Christian Counselors, p. 4.

[5] H. Ray Dunning, *A Layman's Guide to Sanctification* (Kansas City: Beacon Hill Press, 1991), p. 48.

[6] J. Kenneth Grider, *Entire Sanctification: The Distinctive Doctrine of Wesleyanism* (Kansas City: Beacon Hill Press, 1980), p. 25.

[7] Grider, *Entire Sanctification*, p. 60.

[8] Dunning, *A Layman's Guide*, p. 42.

[9] Dunning, *A Layman's Guide*, pp. 72,73, emphasis mine.

[10] George Shaw, *The Spirit in Redemption* (Cincinnati: Press of Jennings and Graham, 1910), p. 147, emphasis mine.

[11] A. M. Hills, *Holiness and Power* (Noblesville: Newby Book Room, 1897), pp. 17,18.

[12] Hills, *Holiness and Power*, pp. 20,21.

[13] Hills, *Holiness and Power*, pp. 20, 21.

[14] Lloyd John Ogilvie, *Drumbeat of Love* (Waco: Word Books, 1976), p. 31.

[15] Taylor, *Life in the Spirit*, p. 123.

[16] Ogilvie, *Drumbeat*, p. 15.

[17] Charles Colson, *Loving God* (Grand Rapids: Zondervan Publishing House, 1983), p. 172.

[18] Colson, *Loving God*, p. 170.

[19] Elizabeth Elliot, *Shadow of the Almighty* (New York: Harper & Brothers, 1958), p. 89.

## Chapter Six

[1] Calvin Miller, *Taste of Joy* (Downer's Grove: Inter-Varsity Press, 1983), p. 24.

[2] Miller, *Taste of Joy*, p. 58.

[3] Charles Caldwell Ryrie, *Balancing The Christian Life* (Chicago: Moody Press, 1969), p. 9.

[4] W. Graham Scroggie, *The Unfolding Drama of Redemption* (Grand Rapids: Zondervan Publishing House, 1976) p. 33.

[5] Henry Blackaby & Claude King, *Experiencing God* (Nashville: Broadman & Holman Publishers, 1994), p. 96.

[6] Oletta Wald, *The Joy of Discovery* (Minneapolis: Augsburg Publishing House, 1975), p. 8.

[7] Douglas Groothuis, *The Soul in Cyberspace* (Grand Rapids: Baker Books, 1997), p. 146.

[8] R. A. Torrey, *How to Study the Bible* (New Kensington: Whitaker House, 19850, p. 17.

[9] Torrey, *Study the Bible*, pp. 17, 18.

[10] *The Navigator Bible Studies Handbook* (Colorado Springs: NavPress, 1994), p. 11.

[11] Becky Benenate & Joseph Durepos, ed. *Mother Teresa: No Greater Love* (Novato: New World Library, 1997), pp. 4, 5.

[12] Wesley Duewell, *Touch the World Through Prayer* (Grand Rapids: Francis Asbury Press, 1986), p. 21.

[13] Duewel, *Touch the World*, p. 25.

[14] Duewel, *Touch*, pp. 13, 14.

[15] Ronald J. Sider, *Living Like Jesus* (Grand Rapids: Baker Books, 1996), p. 59.

[16] Sider, *Living Like Jesus, p. 62.*

[17] Anonymous Author, *The Kneeling Christian* (Grand Rapids: Zondervan Publishing House, 1971), p. 12, emphasis mine.

[18] Eileen Egan, Kathleen Egan, eds., *Prayertimes With Mother Teresa* (New York: Image Books, 1989), pp. 1–4.

[19] C. Welton Gaddy, *A Love Affair With God* (Nashville: Broadman and Holman Publishers, 1995), p. 103.

[20] Jack R. Taylor, *The Hallelujah Factor* (Nashville: Broadman Press, 1983), p. 13.

[21] Gaddy, *A Love Affair,* p. 99.

[22] David Ford, *The Shape of Living* (Grand Rapids: Baker Books, 1997), p. 114.

[23] Gaddy, *Love Affair,* p. 99.

[24] Gaddy, p. 84.

[25] Gaddy, p. 110.

[26] Gaddy, p. 143.

[27] Dallas Willard, *The Spirit of the Disciplines* (San Francisco: Harper Collins, 1988), p. 158.

[28] Richard J. Foster, *Celebration of Discipline* (San Francisco: Harper & Row, 1988), p. 1.

[29] Foster, *Celebration*

[30] Miller, *Taste of Joy*, p. 20.

[31] Willard, *Spirit of Disciplines, pp. 16,17.*

[32] Richard Shelley Taylor, *The Disciplined Life* (Kansas City: Beacon Hill Press, 1962), p. 11.

[33] Willard, *Spirit of Disciplines, p. 126.*

[34] Willard, *Spirit of Disciplines, pp. xi, xii.*

[35] Philip Yancey, "Living With Furious Opposites," *Christianity Today*, September 4, 2000, p. 73.

[36] Willard, *Spirit of Disciplines*, p. xii.

**Chapter Seven**

[1] David L. McKenna, *Growing Up in Christ* (Indianapolis: Light and Life Communications, 1998), p. 107.

[2] Wesley Tracy, et al., *The Upward Call* (Kansas City: Beacon Hill Press, 1994), p. 137.

[3] Tracy, et al, *Upward Call*, p. 135, emphasis mine.

[4] Tracy, et al *Upward Call*, pp. 138,139.

[5] Tracy, et al *Upward Call*, p. 139.

[6] Ronald J. Sider, *Living Like Jesus,* (Grand Rapids: Baker Books, 1996), p. 81.

[7] Douglas Groothuis, *The Soul in Cyberspace* (Grand Rapids: Baker Books, 1997), pp. 16,17, emphasis mine.

[8] Groothuis, p. 125.

[9] Francis A. Schaeffer, *A Christian Manifesto* (Westchester: Crossway Books, 1981), p. 51.

[10] George Barna, *The Frog in the Kettle* (Ventura: Regal Books, 1990), p. 79.

[11] Elton Trueblood, *The Company of the Committed* (New York: Harper & Row, 1961), p. 69.

[12] C. William Fisher, *You'll Like Being a Christian* (Kansas City: Beacon Hill Press, 1971) pp. 9, 10.


**Chapter Eight**

[1] Edith Schoeffer, *What Is a Family?* (Old Tappan: Fleming H. Revell Co., 1975), p. 32.

[2] Schaeffer, *What is a Family?*, p. 32.

[3] Schaeffer, *What is a Family?*, pp. 50,51.

[4] A. J. Russell, ed., *God Calling* (New York: Dodd, Mead & Company, 1958), p. 23.

[5] Dallas Willard, *The Spirit of the Disciplines* (San Francisco: Harper Collins, 1988), p. 259.

[6] John F. Kennedy, Address before National Football Foundation

[7] Elton Trueblood, "A Time for Holy Dissatisfaction," *Leadership* (Winter, 1983), p. 19.

[8] Oswald Chambers, *Approved Unto God* (Grand Rapids: Discovery House Publishers, 1997), p. 73.

[9] E. A. Girvin, *Phineas F. Bresee: A Prince in Israel* (Kansas City: Nazarene Publishing House, 1916), p. 164.

[10] A. W. Tozer, *The Root of The Righteous* (Harrisburg: Christian Publications, Inc., 1955), p. 9.

[11] Elton Trueblood, *The Company of the Committed* (New York: Harper & Row, 1961), p. 31.

[12] Trueblood, *Company*, p. 38.


**Chapter Nine**

[1] James Lee West, "Get the Mail Out," *Frontlines*, April, 2000, p. 4.

[2] Eugene Peterson's *The Message*.

[3] Francis Schaeffer, *The Church at the End of the 20th Century* (Downer's Grove: Inter-Varsity Press, 1970), pp. 133, 134.

[4] Josh McDowell, "Truth and Tolerance," *Focus on the Family*, August, 1999, p. 7.

[5] Mildred Wynkoop, *A Theology of Love* (Kansas City: Beacon Hill Press, 1972), p. 23.

[6] Wynkoop, *Theology of Love*, p. 25.

[7] Charles Colson, *Kingdoms in Conflict* (Grand Rapids: Morrow & Zondervan, 1987), p. 365.

[8] John R. W. Stott, *Basic Christianity* (Grand Rapids: William B. Eerdmans Publishing Company, 1972), p. 141.

[9] Kenneth Chafin, *Is There A Family in the House?* (Waco: Word Books, 1978), p. 16.

[10] James Dobson,

[11] Edith Schaeffer, *What is a Family?* (Old Tappan: Fleming H. Revell Company, 1975), p. 37.

[12] John Whitehead, *Christians Involved in the Political Process* (Chicago: Moody, 1994), p. 5.

[13] Charles Colson, *The Role of the Church in Society* (Wheaton: Victor Books, 1986), p. 7.

[14] Francis Schaeffer, *A Christian Manifesto* (Westchester: Crossway Books, 1981), p. 56.

[15] Glen Tinder, *The Political Meaning of Christianity* (San Francisco: HarperCollins, 1991), pp. 164, 199.

[16] Doug Bandow *Beyond Good Intentions: A Biblical View of Politics* (Wheaton: Crossway Books, 1988), p. 163.

[17] Whitehead, *Christians Involved*, p. 29.

[18] Whitehead, p. 28.

[19] Whitehead, p. 58.

[20] Robert Dugan, *Stand and Be Counted* (Sisters: Multnomah Books, 1995), p. 59.

[21] Dugan, *Stand*, p. 62.

[22] Rabbi Daniel Lapin, *America's Real War* (Sisters: Multnomah, 1999), p. 359.

[23] Charles Colson, *Kingdoms in "Conflict* (Morrow-Zondervan, 1987), p. 371.


**Chapter Ten**

[1] C. S. Lewis, *The Problem of Pain* (New York: Macmillan Publishing Co., 1962), p. 7.

[2] Dietrich Bonhoeffer, *The Cost of Discipleship* (New York: Macmillan Publishing Co., 1979), p. 99.

[3] Michael Molinos, *The Spiritual Guide* (Sargent: Seedsowers, 1972), p. 38.

[4] Oswald Chambers, *If Thou Wilt Be Perfect* (Ft. Washington: Christian Literature Crusade, 1973), pp. 108, 109.

[5] Lewis, *Problem of Pain*, p. 41.

[6] Philip Yancey, "Living With Furious Opposites," *Christianity Today*, September 4, 2000, p. 81.

[7] Yancey, *Opposites*, p. 73.

[8] Oswald Chambers, *Not Knowing Whither* (Basingstoke: Marshall, Morgan, & Scott, 1975), p. 112.

[9] J. Heinrich Arnold, *Discipleship* (Farmington: The Plough Publishing House, 1994), p. 72.

[10] Yancey, *Opposites*, p. 73.

[11] E. Stanley Jones, *A Song of Ascents* (Nashville: Abingdon, 1979, p. 89.

[12] David Ford, *The Shape of Living* (Grand Rapids: Baker Books, 1997), pp. 168, 169.

[13] Glaphre, *When The Pieces Don't Fit God Makes the Difference* (Grand Rapids: Zondervan, 1984), p. 106.

[14] Glaphre, *Pieces,* p. 91.

[15] Calvin Miller, *The Taste of Joy* (Downer's Grove: Inter-Varsity Press, 1983), p. 16.

[16] Ford, *Shape of Living,* p. 166.

[17] Stan Meek, "How to Pray for Healing," *How to Improve Your Prayer Life,* ed. Stephen Miller (Kansas City: Beacon Hill Press, 1987), p. 68.

[18] Ford, *Shape,* 159.

[19] Ford, *Shape,* 173.

[20] Becky Benenate & Joseph Durepos, *Mother Teresa: No Greater Love* (Novato: New World Library, 1997), p. 137.

[21] Yancey, *Opposites,* p. 71.

[22] Charles Colson, *How Now Shall We Live* (Wheaton: Tyndale House Publishers, Inc., 1999), p. 52.

[23] William A. Dembski, ed., *Mere Creation* (Downer's Grove: Inter-Varsity Press, 1998), p. 449.

[24] Dembski, *Mere Creation,* pp. 16, 17.

[25] Dembski, *Mere Creation,* p. 114.

[26] Dembski, *Mere Creation,* p. 140.

[27] Colson, *How Shall We Live,* p. 69.

[28] Colson, *How Shall We Live,* p. 79.

[29] Gene Edward Veith, *Postmodern Times* (Wheaton: Crossway Books, 1994), pp. 192,193.

[30] Os Guinness, *The Gravedigger's File* (Downer's Grove: Inter-Varsity Press, 1983), p. 96.

[31] Veith, *Postmodern Times,* p. 193.

[32] Guinness, *Gravedigger's File,* p. 103.

[33] Guinness, *Gravedigger's File,* p. 98.

[34] Veith, *Postmodern Times,* pp. 68, 69.

[35] Veith, *Postmodern Times,* pp. 68, 69.

[36] John Bunyan, *Pilgrim's Progress* (Grand Rapids: Zondervan Publishing House, 1996), p. 75.

[37] Bunyan, *Pilgrim,* p. 78.

[38] Douglas Groothuis, *The Soul in Cyberspace* (Grand Rapids: Baker Books, 1997), p. 78, emphasis mine.

[39] Guinness, *Gravedigger's File,* pp. 237,238.

[40] Michael R. Phillips, ed., *Knowing the Heart of God* (Minneapolis: Bethany House Publishers, 1990), pp. 196,197.

**Chapter Eleven**

[1] Hannah Whitall Smith, *The Christian's Secret of a Happy Life* (Old Tappan: Fleming H. Revell Co., 1979), pp. 90, 91.

[2] Norvall Hadley, *Sin and the Sanctified* (Kansas City: Beacon Hill Press, 1980), p. 51.

[3] W. T. Purkiser, *Interpreting Christian Holiness* (Kansas City: Beacon Hill Press, 1980), p. 51.

[4] Smith, *The Christian's Secret,* p. 92.

[5] Smith, *The Christian's Secret,* p. 94.

[6] Smith, *The Christian's Secret,* p. 93.

[7] C. Neil Strait, *To Be Holy* (Kansas City: Beacon Hill Press, 1984), p. 53.

[8] Calvin Miller, *The Taste of Joy* (Downer's Grove: Inter-Varsity Press, 1983), p. 18.

[9] Miller, *Taste of Joy*, p. 21.

[10] Douglas Groothuis, *The Soul in Cyberspace* (Grand Rapids: Baker Books, 1997), p. 15.

[11] Groothuis, p. 82.

[12] Dwight Hervey Small, *The High Cost of Holy Living* (Westwood: Fleming H. Revell Co., 1954), p. 9.


**Chapter Twelve**

[1] C. S. Lewis quote from "Caring for People God's Way," *External Divisions Catalong (American* Association of Christian Counselors, p. 4.

[2] Ken Blanshard, *The Heart of a Leader* (Tulsa: Honor Books, 1999), p. 152.

[3] George Barna, *Turning Vision Into Action* (Ventura: Regal, 1996), p. 50.

[4] Barna, *Vision*, p. 117.

[5] Barna, p. 16.

[6] Barna, p. 44.

[7] Barna, p. 68.

[8] Barna, p. 115.

[9] Barna, p. 36.

[10] Barna, p. 14.

[11] Barna, pp. 62,63.

[12] Barna, p. 65

[13] Barna, p. 50.

[14] Oswald Chambers, *Not Knowing Whither* (Basingstoke: Marshall, Morgan, and Scott, 1975), pp. 56, 57.

[15] Henry Blackaby, *Experiencing God* (Nashville: Broadman & Holman Publishers, 1994), p. 271.

[16] Chambers, *Not Knowing, p. 149.*

[17] Becky Benenate & Joseph Dureopos, *Mother Teresa: No Greater Love* (Novato: New World Library, 1997), pp. 29, 30.

[18] Benenate, *Mother Teresa*, p. 87.

[19] Dave W. Breese, *Discover Your Destiny* (Waco: Word Books, 1965), p. 92.

[20] Oswald Chambers, *If Thou Wilt Be Perfect* (Ft. Washington: Christian Literature Crusade, 1973), p. 111.

[21] Chambers, *Not Knowing*, p. 92.


**Chapter Thirteen**

[1] Oswald Chambers, *Not Knowing Whither* (Basingstoke: Marshall, Morgan & Scott, 1975), p. 31.

[2] Elton Trueblood, *Confronting Christ* (Waco: Word Books, 1960), pp. 94, 96.

[3] Chambers, *Not Knowing*, p. 126.

[4] Chambers, *Not Knowing*, p. 126.

[5] David L. McKenna, *Growing Up in Christ* (*Indianapolis:* Light and Life Communications, 1998), p. 138.

[6] McKenna, *Growing Up, pp. 138, 139.*

[7] Dietrich Bonhoeffer, *The Cost of Discipleship* (New York: Macmillan Publishing Co., 1979), p. 320.

[8] McKenna, *Growing Up*, p. 139.

[9] Jon Johnston, *Christian Excellence* (Kansas City: Nazarene Publishing House, 1985), p. 79.

[10] Eileen Egan & Kathleen Egan, *Prayertimes With Mother Teresa* (New York: Image Books, 1989), p. 4.

[11] Egan, *Prayertimes*, p. 25.

[12] John Bunyan, *The Pilgrim's Progress*, (Grand Rapids: Zondervan Publishing House, 1966), pp. 65, 66.

[13] Keith Phillips, *The Making of a Disciple* (Old Tappan: Fleming H. Revell Company, 1981), p. 34.


**Chapter Fourteen**

[1] Calvin Miller, *Taste of Joy* (Downer's Grove: Inter-Varsity Press, 1983), p. 88.

[2] J. I. Packer, *Knowing God* (Downer's Grove: Inter-Varsity Press, 1973), p. 29.

[3] Oswald Chambers, *Not Knowing Whither* (Basingstoke: Marshall, Morgan, and Scott, 1975), p. 126.

[4] Packer, *Knowing God*, p. 32.

[5] Packer, pp. 14, 15.

[6] Packer, p. 198.

[7] John MacArthur, *The Glory of Heaven* (Wheaton: Crossway Books, 1996), p. 142.

[8] MacArthur, *Glory of Heaven*, p. 187.

[9] December, 2000 Newsletter from Wycliffe Associates, Orange, CA.

[10] MacArthur, *Glory of Heaven*, pp. 187, 188.

[11] MacArthur, p. 68.

[12] Ralph Earle, *Behold I Come* (Kansas City: Beacon Hill Press, 1973), p. 75.
[13] MacArthur, *Glory,* p. 68.
[14] John Piper, *Future Grace* (Sisters: Multnomah Books, 1995), p. 20.

**Chapter Fifteen**

[1] Harry E. Jessop, *Foundations of Doctrine* (Chicago: The Chicago Evangelistic Institute, 1944), p. 55.
[2] Jessop, *Foundations,* p. 56.

# APPENDIX

# A SUGGESTED READING LIST FOR DISCIPLES

There are thousands of good books. It is impossible for any one to list all of the books that a disciple of Christ should read. A book that touches one person deeply may hardly register on another. There are some books which have touched enough people over a long enough period of time to become known as "classics." It is the author's opinion that a suggested reading list should include both classics and contemporary writings. The following list simply includes some of the books that have influenced the author's life.

## For Personal Spiritual Formation

*Approved Unto God* by Oswald Chambers
*Celebration of Discipline* by Richard Foster
*Cost of Discipleship, The,* by Dietrich Bonhoeffer
*Christian Manifesto, The,* by Francis Schaeffer
*Experiencing God,* by Henry Blackaby
*Gold Cord* by Amy Carmichael
*How Should We Then Live,* by Francis Schaeffer
*How Now Shall We Live,* by Charles Colson

*Knowing God*, by J. I. Packer
*Living Like Jesus*, by Ron Sider
*Loving God*, by Charles Colson
*Love Affair With God, A*, C. Welton Gaddy
*Making All Things New*, by Henri Nouwen
*Mother Teresa: No Greater Love*, ed. by Becky Benenate & Joseph Durepos
*Man, The Dwelling Place of God*, by A. W. Tozer

*My Utmost for His Highest*, by Oswald Chambers
*The Normal Christian Life*, by Watchman Nee
*Pilgrim's Progress* by John Bunyan
*Place of Help, The*, by Oswald Chambers
*Pursuit of God, The*, by A. W. Tozer
*Root of the Righteous, The*, by A. W. Tozer
*Shadow of The Almighty, The Life and Testament of Jim Elliot*, by Elizabeth Elliot
*Shape of Living, The*, by David Ford
*Song of Ascents, The*, by E. Stanley Jones
*Spirit of the Disciplines, The*, by Dallas Willard
*Spiritual Guide, The*, by Michael Molinos
*Studies in the Sermon on the Mount*, by Oswald Chambers
*Table of Inwardness*, by Calvin Miller
*Taste of Joy*, by Calvin Miller
*That Incredible Christian*, by A. W. Tozer
*True Spirituality*, by Francis Schaeffer

## The Deeper Life or Christian Holiness

*Be Perfect*, by Andrew Murray
*Breath of God, The*, Herbert Lockyer
*Christian Perfection*, by John Wesley
*Christian's Secret of a Happy Life, The*, Hannah Whitall Smith
*Deeper Experiences of Famous Christians*, by James Gilchrist Lawson
*Entire Sanctification*, by J. Kenneth Grider

*Holiness and High Country*, by Albert Harper
*How to Be Filled With the Spirit*, by Richard S. Taylor
*Highest Life, The*, by Gene Edwards
*If Thou Wilt Be Perfect*, by Oswald Chambers
*Interpreting Christian Holiness*, by W. T. Purkiser
*John Wesley's Concept of Perfection*, by Leo Cox
*Layman's Guide to Sanctification, A*, by H. Ray Dunning
*Life in the Spirit*, by Richard S. Taylor
*Scriptural Freedom from Sin*, by Henry Brockett
*Studies in Biblical Holiness*, by Donald Metz
*Upward Call, The*, by Wesley Tracy, and et. al.
*Vision Which Transforms, The*, by George Allen Taylor
*Wholeness in Christ*, by William Greathouse
*Wholly Sanctified*, by A. B. Simpson

## Books on Prayer

*God Listens,* by Samuel Chadwick
*How To Pray*, by R. A. Torrey
*Kneeling Christian, The*, (written by an unknown Christian)
*If You Shall Ask*, by Oswald Chambers
*Little Book About Prayer, A*, by W. E. McCumber
*Prayer Life, The*, by Andrew Murray
*Prevailing Prayer*, by D. L. Moody
*Prayertimes with Mother Teresa*, ed. by Eileen Egan and Kathleen Egan
*Touch the World Through Prayer*, by Wesley Duewel
*With Christ in the School of Prayer*, by Andrew Murray

## Christian Apologetics

*Evidence That Demands a Verdict* by Josh McDowell
*Know What and Why You Believe*, by Paul Little

# BIBLES AND BIBLE HELPS

## English Translations of the Bible

Translating from the original languages has provided us with different kinds of texts: 1) literal translations, which perhaps give the closest idea as to what the original language texts said, 2) dynamic equivalent translations, which are very accurate, but provide more of the thrust and flow of the message, and 3) the looser or freer translations, which become, more or less, paraphrases of the original language texts.

*Examples of literal translations:*

*King James Version*
*Revised Standard Version*
New American Standard Version
American Standard Version

*Popular dynamic equivalent translations:*

*New International Version*

New English Bible
*Today's English Version*

The following scale may be useful to some in picturing where some popular versions fit in the translating scheme.*

| Literal | | dynamic equivalent | | | free |
|---|---|---|---|---|---|
| KJV | RSV | NIV | GNB | PHILLIPS | TLB |
| NASB | | NAB | JB | | |
| | | | NEB | | |

There are many other modern versions of the Bible. A recommended primer on these translations is: *God's Word in Man's Language*, by Robert Branson, Beacon Hill Press, 1980.

## Bible Dictionaries, Concordances, and Handbooks:

*Dictionaries:* (Brief summaries of information, alphabetically arranged, regarding names, places, events and vital subjects.)

*Harper's Bible Dictionary*, ed. By Paul J. Achtemeier
*Interpreter's Dictionary of the Bible*, ed. by George A. Buttrick
*International Standard Bible Encyclopedia* 4 vols., ed by G. W. Bromley,
Eerdmans, 1988
*Nelson's Illustrated Bible Dictionary*, ed. by Herbert Lockyer, Sr.
(an excellent layman's Bible dictionary.)

---

*The scale is from Fee & Stuart's *How to Read the Bible for All It's Worth*. (*Zondervan*, 1982) According to these authors, "The best translational theory is dynamic equivalence. A literal translation is often helpful as a *second* source; it will give you confidence as to what the Greek or Hebrew actually looked like. A free translation also can be helpful to stimulate your thinking about the possible meaning of the text. But the basic translation for reading and studying should be something like the NIV."

*New Bible Dictionary*, ed. J. D. Douglas, Eerdmans, 1962
*Zondervan's Pictorial Encyclopedia of the Bible*, ed. by Merrill C. Tenney,
Zondervan, 1975.

*Handbooks:*

*Eerdman's Handbook to the Bible*, by David and Patricia Alexander

*Bible Concordances:*

A useful tool in discovering the occurrence of a given word in various passages of Scripture. "Exhaustive," or "Complete" concordances will list every appearance of every word in the Bible. Perhaps the three best known concordances are *Strong's, Young's, and Cruden's.* Some concordances are keyed to particular versions of the Bible, and many Bibles have limited concordances within their covers.

*Nave's Topical Bible,* Bible references that relate to various topics.

*Bible Commentaries:*

Notes by Bible scholars can help in understanding and interpreting specific verses or passages of Scripture. The problem here is that there is a wide variety of types of commentaries, from a basically devotional type to the highly theological type. So one must consider what his or her purpose is in Bible study when choosing a commentary.

*The Daily Study Bible* by Westminster Press contains 24 volumes on the Old Testament. These are written by a variety of scholars. The New Testament contains 17 volumes, all by William Barclay. Excellent, philological, historical, and literary content for the student or teacher.

There are many one-volume commentaries such as *The Wycliffe Bible Commentary*, ed, by Charles Pfeiffer and Everett Harrison.

*Bible Interpretation:* (How to read and study the Bible)

*How to Read the Bible for All It's Worth*, by Gordon Fee and Douglas Stuart.

*The Joy of Discovery in Bible Study*, by Oletta Wald.

*The Navigator's Bible Studies Handbook* by Navpress.

## Abbreviations of Translations

| | |
|---|---|
| GNB | The Good News Bible (formerly Today's English Version), 1976 |
| JB | The Jerusalem Bible, 1966. |
| KJV | The King James Version (also known as the Authorized Version), 1611 |
| TLB | The Living Bible, 1971. |
| NAB | The New American Bible, 1970 |
| NASB | The New American Standard Bible, 1960. |
| NEB | The New English Bible, 1961. |
| NIV | The New International Version, 1973. |
| RSV | The Revised Standard Version, 1952. |

# A SIMPLE PLAN FOR LEADING A PERSON TO CHRIST

There are many different plans for seeking to lead a friend or loved one into a personal relationship with Christ. *Witnessing* may be as simple as sharing "your story"—telling what Jesus did for **you**. One can explain what his or her life was like before accepting Jesus, and what it is like now. The simple telling of your story can be used by God to stimulate interest. It is a seed that is sown.

There are times, however, when one may feel that the person being witnessed to is ready to take a more definite step toward Christ. They may need only a little nudge toward taking the most important step of their lives. Here is a simple, Scriptural plan for helping such a person:

A good Scripture verse to begin with is Revelation 3:20. "Here I am! I stand at the door and knock. If anyone hears my voice and opens the door, I will come in and eat with him, and he with me."

Explain that Jesus is standing at the door of every person's heart. He does not ever "crash" the door down or make a forced entry. He lovingly knocks and softly calls out our name. Because He respects our self-sovereignty, He patiently waits to be invited in. (One might even use a small picture of Salman's painting which shows Christ standing at a door and knocking.)

One can personalize this plan, by asking questions like, "What do you think the door stands for?" "What does Christ say He wants us to do here?" "Who does Christ appear to be talking to here?" Involving the person in this way will make it easier for them to feel they have indeed made their own deductions, decisions, and commitments.

The focus can then be shifted to Christ's promise—what He promises to do for those who open the door. His promise, of course, is *that He will come in and eat a fellowship meal with them.* Here, one can emphasize the joy we have when sharing a meal with those we love. The greatest *feast* of all is when we have intimate fellowship with God through Christ.

At this point, the focus can be shifted to *how one opens that door.* The preceding verse (19) tells us how. It is through *repentance.* But since Jesus introduces the subject within the framework of His love, there will ordinarily be less resistance and objection to the subjects of *sin* and *repentance.*

Appropriate Scriptures to use here might be Romans 3:10, Romans 3:23, Romans 6:23 and Romans 5:8. (these are all in Romans, and have been known as the Roman Road to Salvation) Other Scriptures that might be helpful are 1 John 1:9, and Proverbs 28:13.

These Scriptures can be used to help prepare the seeker's heart to pray and ask Christ to come into their heart.

Often a seeker will need help in offering this prayer. You can invite them to pray a simple prayer following your own words, or to pray their own prayer. It is important once they have prayed that prayer and opened their hearts to Jesus, to help them feel assurance about it.

Ask them, "Did you open the door of your heart and invite Jesus in?" "What did Jesus promise to do if we opened the door?" "Then where is Jesus right now, according to His own Word?" A couple of verses that help with assurance are found in 1 John 5: 11 and 12, "And this is the testimony: God has given us eternal life, and this life is in His Son. He who has the Son has life, he who does not have the Son does not have life." Assure the seeker that whoever opens the door to Jesus has eternal life, because Jesus is "the way, the truth, and the Life."

It is important not only to pray with the person again at this point, thanking God for their courage in praying to accept Christ, but also praying directly for them to be true and to walk in the light God gives them. Pray for them to read God's Word, to cultivate a prayer life, and to attend church faithfully.

Finally, it is helpful if one can secure a commitment from the new Christian that they will tell someone what God has done for them. One can ask if they mind if you share with their pastor what they have done, and, even more important, if they mind if the pastor shares with the congregation on Sunday morning about their new start with God.

Handled properly by you and your pastor, this can be not only a strengthening of the new convert's faith, but a great blessing and help to the whole congregation.

To order additional copies of

Have your credit card ready and call

**Toll free: (877) 421-READ (7323)**

or send $13.99* each plus $5.95 S&H** to

WinePress Publishing
PO Box 428
Enumclaw, WA 98022

or order online at: www.winepressbooks.com

*WA residents, add 8.4% sales tax

**add $1.50 S&H for each additional book ordered